Everything You Will Ever Need To Know To Start

Driving A Big Truck

Or

How I Became A Professional Tourist

Steve Richards

Outskirts Press, Inc.
Denver, Colorado

Everything You Will Ever Need To Know To Start Driving A Big Truck Or How I Became A Professional Tourist

Outskirts Press
http://www.outskirtspress.com

ISBN-10: 1-59800-616-9
ISBN-13: 978-1-59800-616-2

Table Of Contents

Introduction

Perhaps you are one of those people who has never left the place you were born and have little intention of ever doing so. You have little interest in seeing the rest of the country, in finding what is out there in the "real world," or seeing what you might be missing. You will live and die right in the same small space you have always occupied and the town you have always lived in, going to work at the same boring office, store, or warehouse you have gone to every day for countless years. Nothing is ever new to you.

Every night you will sit on the couch watching those stunning "reality shows," scintillating police docudramas, and stellar sitcoms on the idiot box. Maybe you can be a big winner on "Jeopardy" and some day you're going to win the lottery too. And, on your day off you will occasionally spring for a big night out on the town, spending half of what you made the previous week and later regretting it.

There are millions of people just like that. Are you one? Is that really how you want to spend your existence? I have met many such folks and am always astounded by the fact that their lives lack any sense of adventure or even a remote semblance of intellectual curiosity. So many people are content to just exist and accept that all they can ever be is what they already are. If that is you then by all means I say "good luck and be happy." Someone who is not interested in seeing what is out there, probably never will be any more than they already are. Such a shame.

People such as this are missing one of the most incredible opportunities available in the free society in which we live. It is life. Get out and live it. **See the sights**. Be an explorer. Expand your horizons and **get paid to do it**. Yes, you too can actually get paid to be on a virtually endless vacation.

How often do you drive down the road and see people who have spent a veritable fortune to obtain a large motor home, or maybe they have a huge camper trailer attached to the back of their pickup, and on top of that there is actually another car hooked to the back of that trailer? Sometimes it looks absolutely absurd, until you watch them try to drive it. Then there is no doubt as to the absurdity. Ah yes, that's the way to do it.

These "happy campers" work all year long so they can take a week or two to go traveling about the country. With the cost of gas, tires, and vehicle maintenance, on top of the tremendous amount spent to obtain and insure their "happy little houses on wheels," it seems a shame that they only have such a short time to see the sights before returning to their relatively dull day to day lives. Sounds like a stress free way to travel, or **not!**

Or, perhaps you are one of those truly unlucky folks who says, "Too bad we won't ever have the money to buy one of those fancy rides, let alone ever be able to afford a real vacation." Maybe you are someone who has lost your job and don't have any money at all. "Are you nuts?" You say, "Forget the vacation. I can't even pay the bills and afford to eat." This is the reality for many folks!

Life is short enough and with so little time available to do the things you really want, along with the necessity of a job to pay the bills, it can become essential to combine certain aspects of your life. Why not get paid to be on a perpetual vacation? You don't have to fight the endless daily traffic grind to get to your job.

You can roll right out of the rack, grab your coffee, take two steps, sit down in the driver's seat, and you are ready to go to work. Shut off the brakes, put it in gear, let the clutch out, roll it, and you are makin' bank, dudes. "Uhhh, what?"

A "big truck," in case you are confused, is one of those terrifying and gigantic tractor trailer monstrosities (clocking in at seventy-one feet or so and with a weight of up to 80,000 pounds), that pervade the highways across America, supposedly wreaking havoc, as so many are convinced, upon all who dare to get in the way of progress. "Get out of my way now, or be crushed into oblivion, you moron!" Just a little levity. You don't really want to run over that nice little minivan. Do you? Uhhh, you might need to think about that for a second.

A "professional tourist" can be a driver of the aforementioned who is not just there to transport frozen vegetables back and forth across the interstates, but can in fact be one who is well paid year round to see and experience the incredible sights. You are always on vacation and you are always in charge of what you will be doing.

This discussion is going to fully divulge to those who have ever even considered driving a big rig, or just to anyone who might be curious as to what actually goes on in the world of trucking, in English (no high level, incomprehensible, trucker CB terminology required), precisely every little thing you will ever need to know to get rollin' and to even find some of the most amazing and unique jobs in transportation. There it is, and all in one long sentence.

As someone who started driving seven years ago, and as one who has no intention whatsoever of donating my entire life to the world of trucking, or my services to any one transportation company for an extended period, this book encompasses much of my personal experience and extensive observational skill. "Kill me baby," but I do know what the hell I am talking about.

You do not need to drive for thirty years in order to gain a "firm grasp of the obvious." In fact if you do put in your thirty years, and hopefully not with the same company, I think it is possible to completely lose touch with reality. It does happen and with frequency. Once you spend a little time listening to drivers philosophically bantering back and forth over their CB radios, you will quickly realize that complete sanity and even lucidity of speech are not pre-requisites in the world of eighteen wheelers.

As time goes by truck drivers do tend to see the world a bit differently. When you are out on the road and you start talking to yourself, that's ok, as long as you don't answer back. And with regularity, you will start talking to yourself.

While all this newly acquired freedom and adventure can become a truly monumental part of your existence, unless you absolutely love it, it is not my recommendation, that you spend your whole life on the highway. Perhaps once you have seen it all several times, that may prove to be enough. Who knows?

Just get out and see the sights and get paid to do it. See the whole U.S. and in fact the whole North American Continent if you are so desirous. I will in these pages show you that unequivocally there is absolutely nothing complicated about this. Once you learn the ropes there is no limit to where you can take it.

There is no unemployment in the transportation industry and the availability of these positions is nearly infinite. There are driver recruiters all over the country waiting to beg you to take a position with the companies they represent. However caution is advised here, because as with many things, they are not always as they appear. We will explore these eventualities later in a bit more detail.

Though let me put this in overly simplistic terms. If you are a homeless bum on the streets without a penny to your name, you can literally walk up to a pay phone, dial the infamous 800 toll free number, and express an interest in driving a "big truck." After that, you can walk into nearly any library, get on one of their free for anybody Internet access computers, fill out an online job application, and within days be whisked off to a distant city of your choice, where you will in fact be instructed in the fine art of the operation of a big rig. Yes, nearly anyone can do this.

This is a bit simplified and yet not really. It is in reality that simple and amazing that more people don't take advantage of this remarkable opportunity. Oh, they may want to send you a bus ticket or they may actually fly you first class to their destination, and entirely at their expense. There are differences and similarities in all transportation companies, but generally, this is how it all starts.

The fact that I have worked for quite a few of these transportation entities, both big and small, and in a relatively short period of time, does make me somewhat of an expert on what you will be getting into and what you can expect. I have never stayed too long with any one company, and while that may be a negative in many lines of work, it is a matter of variety for me. I have always enjoyed new experiences and there are many of them to be lived in the world of big trucks. Additionally, there are few things as satisfying as saying goodbye and walking away from a company of which you are happy to be free. Yeah!

Rest assured, I am well versed on this subject and one is unlikely to come upon such information elsewhere. I have looked, and while I am occasionally privileged to a tidbit of interest, it is not the norm. In the words of Howard Cosell, I will "tell it like it is." Driving a big truck is not just for mutant buffoons incapable of otherwise securing employment. While such evil miscreants are prevalent in the industry, they are also mostly avoidable with a little effort. In reality you may even come upon an educated truck driver, one with a brain, and the capability to carry on an intelligent conversation unrelated to the load of pork widgets, that he is hauling to Nacogdoches. It could happen. Couldn't it?

This is also **not** going to be a literary espousal on the detailed virtues of disconnecting your fifth wheel from your trailer and pulling out, before lowering your landing gear and disconnecting the glad hands. Such essentials are to be learned in trucking school or from your new company, both of whom do indeed have a vested interest in your **not** performing such a task.

While certain essential aspects of the safe and potentially life saving operation of your eighteen wheeler, along with numerous observations of the realities of the trucking world will be emphasized here, this is not the essence of this work. I have no interest whatsoever in teaching anyone how to drive a big rig. That is far beyond the scope of this endeavor or any possible desires to which I have ever fallen prey. It ain't gonna happen here, and that is my 100% guarantee. No thank you. I have never entertained a single thought in regard to my potential as a driver trainer. It is not for me and never ever shall it become so.

What you will get here, you will not likely find in any other publication. In other words, there are things that truck companies do not want their drivers to know lest they become discouraged and not want to drive or be affiliated with their organization. If it has any relevance, it will be covered here and not covered up.

There are numerous obstacles to be dealt with in the world of big trucks, but the majority of them come about due to the fact that, "Nobody ever told me that this would happen." If you know in advance, it can make any potential aggravations substantially easier to deal with. Trust me on that. It is much better to be aware of the oncoming train before you get in the tunnel. Unfortunately in the world of trucking, too many things of importance are either not fully explained to my satisfaction or they are just altogether neglected. If they are not discussed here then they are not important. As I said, this is "Every Thing You Will Ever Need To Know...." and that's the way it is gonna be.

I do get relatively disgusted at people that complain about their employment prospects. "Uhhh, I can't find me no job and um gonna lose the house cuz uh can't pay them bills." Are you a complete fool? There is no excuse for that. This is an absurdly simple process. You aren't too old. You aren't too fat and you aren't too much of a klutz to handle it. If you can read these lines, you aren't too stupid to do this stuff. Male or female, it is of no consequence. There are very few good excuses. Just about anyone is capable of handling this new life and if you do it right you can have a rollicking good time in the process. Don't miss out.

Every year thousands of confused folks enter the transportation industry in search of a new life. The vast majority either does not stick with it for very long, or they end up job hopping in order to find the right company, and rarely do. This is an industry always in search of drivers and one which really makes a pathetic attempt to attract and retain new talent.

Everything you need to know is right here in this exciting and compelling endorsement on a thrill packed journey into your potentially new life on the highway. Pay close attention as this riveting adventure unfolds in all its glory. It is all of the essence and the importance of rereading the contents herein can not be stressed enough.

This is essentially a definitive compendium of survival and success over evidential adversity in the world of big rigs. Seriously though, all you have to do is be willing to "Jump" right in and become a "professional tourist." Read on and learn what it takes to become happily involved with a new opportunity!

Getting Started

Getting Started

1. Getting Your Mind Right

The first thing you will need to consider before jumping into a new career as a professional tourist is, "Can I really do this?" The answer to this is most likely affirmative, but depending on your personal situation it will require several major changes in the way you do things. Make no mistake about it, traveling about the planet in a big rig, is something completely different than that to which you have grown accustomed. It will initially take you right out of your normal comfort zone and for a time cause you to frequently ask, "What am I doing here? This is insanity!"

If you are indeed one of those folks that is not tied to a family situation (wife, kids, mortgage, etc.) things can be quite simple. The changes can be made quickly and smoothly. If you have ever looked, there are thousands of storage facilities about the country that are more than willing to lock up all your worldly possessions and will even provide storage for your personal vehicle for a monthly fee. This is the easiest way to hit the road.

When you are starting out you are going to be traveling non-stop for an extended period. The last thing you need to be worried about is who is breaking into your apartment or house in Denver, when you are down delivering insulation in Nacogdoches, Texas. By the way, have you ever been to Nacogdoches? Drive a truck long enough and there will be very few places that you haven't seen and some of them many times.

There are numerous minor obstacles to be dealt with in "getting started" in your new lifestyle, but none as important as what to do with all your stuff. That is what makes the local storage facility essential to a new driver's success in getting started. They are easy to check in and out of, and that comfort level of knowing that your gold bars and diamonds will still be where you left them when you return is relaxing to say the least.

You will need to keep your mind on the highway and not be concerned with what you left behind. Even more precisely, as a professional tourist the point is to enjoy what is in front of you and forget about that which you left behind (except for your truck mirrors, which we will cover in great detail down the road apiece).

When I started out in trucking I had a very sharp 1988 Corvette, that I did not want to leave behind to deteriorate in some storage lot. What did I do? I put it on consignment at the local Corvette dealer and sold it a couple weeks after getting in the trucking biz. I really enjoyed that car, but it is strictly a possession and such things can be replaced.

One thing you will notice after driving a bit is that it is amazing how you really can get along without all those day to day items that you previously thought to be essential to your survival. The day I parted ways, after a year with my first trucking company, I literally took a cab back to the same Corvette dealer and a couple hours later drove off with a magnificent 1996 Corvette. Just for the record, driving a Corvette has nothing to do with the world of trucking; it is strictly a personal preference.

I could just as easily have gone out and picked up a happenin' mini-van, OR NOT! I really have nothing against mini-vans, except the ones that see a car length of space between your truck and the next vehicle in front of you, and they decide that it is ok to pull into that space. It is not ok!

Forget the fact that after they carelessly swerve in front of you they are then so close to your front bumper that you can barely see the front half of their vehicle. And, what do you suppose is the first thing they do after pulling in front of you? Why yes, they jam on their brakes to avoid hitting the car in front of them.

The person driving the mini-van has a cigarette in one hand, a cell phone in the other, and a car full of passengers. The mini-van driver generally is completely oblivious to the reality that they were nearly smashed to death by nearly 80,000 lbs of bone crushing, flesh mangling tractor trailer.

The average driver of a four wheeler (big time truck driving terminology) is absolutely clueless, when it comes to driving. They are completely unaware that the big truck behind them CAN NOT STOP as quickly as they can. Perhaps they also assume that they would be in the right if they are hit from behind. Perhaps they think, "if that stupid truck driver hits me from behind, I will sue."

The key point here is, that if one is careless enough to cut in front of a tractor trailer and the truck driver is unable to stop in time, they won't be worrying about lawsuits or who is at fault. They will most likely be squashed like a bug on the wall. They will probably be dead. But enough digression and violence for the moment. This happy little chapter is about "getting started" in the transportation industry. We will thoroughly espouse theories of blood and guts later on. I promise to elaborate further.

Other than putting tooth paste back in the tube, nothing is impossible in getting into a big truck. Forget the tooth paste analogy, other than to say, you better not forget to bring it with you. Proper tooth care on the road is of the essence. In other words, if you just lost a crown or need a root canal at the truck stop in Walcott, Iowa at 2:30 in the morning, and your dentist is in Vista, California, "you are out of luck bud." Amazingly enough, there is in fact a dentist at the world's largest truck stop in Walcott, Iowa. However, he ain't in attendance in the middle of the night. Bet the house on that!

Fortunately for me I didn't need a root canal in Walcott, Iowa, but I did have a crown fall off after eating overcooked rock hard French Fries in Walcott, Iowa. Under these circumstances, you put your nice little expensive crown into an empty plastic film container and put it in a safe place until you can get to the dentist and have it glued back on. There are always solutions to your problems on the road. Sometimes you must be creative.

Getting back to "getting started" and as stated previously, nothing is impossible in getting into a big truck. If you do in fact have other contingencies, they can all be dealt with. A serious discussion with yourself and your family is necessitated in order to decide if this is going to be right for you.

I can state emphatically, that if I was married and had little kids to deal with, choosing a life on the road would be tough. If that is your situation you will have to figure out how often you will be getting home to your family. Thousands of drivers do it, but it can certainly provide complications.

Many truck companies out there tell you what a great family oriented organization they are, and yet when it comes time for you to be home on June 2nd for your daughter's high school graduation ceremony, you may have a bit of a disappointment. When you have to count on a driver dispatcher who has 50 other drivers, to get you home at a specific time, do not hold your breath in anticipation of positive results.

Results do vary along these lines and I would not be an optimist in such a situation. Persistence is required. If you need to be somewhere at a specific time, not only do you need to give these people notice. You may need to repeat yourself many times to achieve the desired result. In other words, remember that line about "the squeaky wheel gets the most grease." Sometimes you have to be annoying in the repetition of your desires.

Repetition is good. It is good for your dispatchers and it is good for you. The more you hear things repeated, the better you will remember. I will repeat several things within these pages, some of which can save your life. I will repeat several things within these pages, some of which can save your life. Got it! Excellent!

There are companies that will let you take your spouse on the road and may even let you train them in the fine art of OTR driving. If you do this, keep in mind you will be together nearly 24 hours a day and in a very confined space. Many folks do this successfully for years and years. I believe that that much closeness with your significant other could be too much for some. As large as some truck cabs are, I never have enough room for all my stuff, let alone try to figure out how to get somebody else's stuff in there too. Although, as I said nothing is impossible here. There are obstacles to be overcome.

If you are married and you go on the road, how will your relationship be affected? When you are away from someone for a week or so at a time, perhaps it can prove stimulating to a relationship. However, if you are gone for months on end, people can tend to grow apart. When you are away from someone for a longer period you start to lead a different life and even become a different person altogether. The one who is out on the highway and "seeing the sights," can easily lose touch with the reality of important issues such as diaper changing, cutting the grass, or just staying on top of the latest castoff from your favorite "Reality TV" show.

When you have been gone a few weeks, will you start to wonder if your spouse is waiting around at home? Or, are they out on the town partying while you are sitting in the back of your truck at some grocery warehouse for ten hours waiting for some "professional forklift operator" to take 20 minutes to pull 20 pallets off your trailer? What is really going on while you are traveling down that long, lonely, dark highway in the middle of the night and out in the middle of nowhere? These are things you need to confront before you jump into OTR. If you think this may be a problem down the road, you are absolutely right. Wondering what is going on at home can literally drive you crazy. If this is the case you better figure it out in advance. Deal with it before it is too late.

If you are in fact saddled with real estate holdings. If you own a residence and you do not have a family to watch over your "stuff," this presents a problem. If you are gone for awhile you need to make it look like you are still there. If not you will be concerned about who is running off with your plasma TV and coin collection. You need good locks on your doors, timers on your lights, maybe an alarm system, and who knows what else. This is not a book on home security, but rather a wake up call to those that wish to tempt fate and see the world through OTR. Plan ahead and avoid the potential for future complications.

If you are going to be away for extended periods, you need to do whatever is necessary to provide consolation to your comfort level. You do not want to be thinking about what is going on at home while you are out enjoying the incredible view of the countryside. The Boy Scout motto is "Be prepared." It definitely applies to the world of an over the road driver. Before you make that leap to become a "professional tourist," preparation is essential.

For me the decisions were uncomplicated. I put everything I owned into a large storage facility. It was convenient and I knew everything was very likely to remain exactly where I left it, along with a little extra dust. And with no immediate family to worry about, you can also save a lot of headaches.

Just because you are traveling constantly, your bills will not stop and the bill collectors will not care that you were in Tampa enjoying the Florida State Fair, when your credit card payment was due. It is not complicated to take care of all of these matters before any problems arise.

How can you pay the bills when you are on the road and don't get the mail with any regularity? First and foremost you must keep track of everything you spend and everything that you owe. Write it down. Hold it right there. One more time we have a bit of repetition. Write it down. You are on the road and you do not want to be thinking about bills all the time. You will forget. You may not give a thought to your cell phone bill, until you suddenly realize it has stopped working and you need to make an important call to get directions to your receiver in downtown Chicago. If you write down what you spend, what you owe and when payment is due, this will add extra points towards keeping you in your comfort level.

The way I prefer to handle such things is to put most of my expenses on one specific credit card. You need to know when payments are due and make sure you take care of it in a timely manner. The credit card company will have no qualms whatsoever about messing up your perfect credit report even though you have had a perfect payment record for the last twenty years. They love you when you pay them, but just mess up one time and see if they don't reward you with a negative mark on your Experian Credit Report.

It is amazing what you can do with just the pay phone at a truck stop (Save your cell minutes for important stuff, like calling your mother). After charging all your monthly expenses on the old credit card, you can call the toll free 800 number and get a list of all your charges for the month, making sure they all match in a comparison to your carefully written list. They will give you a payment mailing address and you will write a check for the balance and get it in the mail at least ten days in advance. You can even arrange for the credit card company to automatically take the money to pay your bill directly from your bank account. I don't care for this option and actually prefer the check in the mail routine.

Sometimes the U.S. mail is remarkably quick in delivery times and yet if you are in Tooele, Utah, and your payment is going to Wilmington, Delaware, you want to be sure and allow extra days for delivery. Once again, the credit card company does not care that you are on vacation. They want their money when it is due and it is of no concern to them that you are out in the middle of nowhere and haven't actually even seen your bill.

Never forget to pay the storage bill. You do not want your stuff going on the auction block while you are sitting at the Wal Mart Distribution Center in Paul's Valley, Oklahoma. Storage facilities regularly auction off entire units full of people's stuff. This will not happen to you because you have written it all down and will always know in advance when a bill is coming due.

While paying the bills on the road can be a problem, it doesn't have to become complicated. You know that old saying, "an ounce of prevention is worth a pound of coffee, or some other such thing." There are numerous ways to deal with this. With a little effort you will arrive at your own solutions. Just be sure and take care of it with plenty of time to spare, and you too shall be allowed to remain in your comfort zone as you barrel down the highway.

No matter how much time and effort you put into figuring solutions to all your problems, you will still have things come up that must be dealt with. However, because you did your advance planning in regard to the majority of these things, nothing will be too complicated. Once you have thoroughly examined your situation, and know you can do this, it is time to really get started.

<u>Getting Started</u>

2. Company Selection & Proper Driver Training

Make no mistake about it, getting the proper driver training and going with the right company can have everything in the world to do with your survival into the golden years. When you are getting started there are many things to deal with, but once you get it all down pat, you can basically do it in your sleep (except of course for your driving, try not to sleep too often while operating your big truck, complications may arise).

Statistics here are irrelevant, but while they say that 50% of all marriages end in divorce, I have also heard it said that a similar percentage of all truck drivers lose their CDL (commercial driver's license) within a year after obtaining it. You do not want that to happen to you, so pay close attention. Once you have it. Protect it. Avoid traffic tickets of any kind and if you get popped, fight it in court. Paying a few bucks to hire an attorney may be well spent, because any indiscretions will be on your record for seven long years.

No tickets and no accidents on your official driving record will guarantee you employment well into your senior years. Having certain infractions on your record will not disqualify you from trucking. It just makes you look like more of a risk. Tickets on your CDL also cost more than your regular license to operate a motor vehicle. You are a professional and more is expected of you. You are held to a higher standard. So, don't mess up.

Obtaining a CDL is very similar in most states. Check with your local driver's license office to get a Commercial

Drivers License Book and all the other particulars. Compared to a normal motor vehicle operator's license, there is quite a bit more to this. There are actually books for sale on the subject of acquiring a CDL. You do not need these. All such information is **free** from your state. You do not have to pay for such things. So, don't waste your money.

The first thing you will be doing is acquiring your learner's permit for the CDL. You can do this on your own, wait until you get to truck driving school, or let your newly found company guide you through the entire process. It is all up to you. I actually had my learner's permit and my first DOT physical before I ever went to driving school, and yes it was paid for by somebody else.

I have only gone through this process in two states, California and Colorado, so if your system in Connecticut is different, then deal with it. It can't be all that complicated. Nothing involved with the CDL process is difficult. Some states do have more and some less written testing involved. As I recall going back a few years, there were in fact more tests required in California than in Colorado.

There are seven or eight written tests for which you can study out of your state's commercial driver's handbook. Nothing complicated here, but a bit of memory work. A lot of this stuff you need to know, so learn it once and chances are good that you will rarely have to deal with it again. There may be a test for air brakes, general CDL knowledge test, and various other tests that you should be able to master before you are allowed to be out on the highway.

In California you are given three chances to pass each of the tests. If you still fail after three tries you are subject to a public flogging. Ok, not really, but if you do not pass after the third time, perhaps you should give up trucking and consider raising ostriches in Zihuatanejo.

The tests cover various aspects of trucking that include any endorsements you may wish to have attached to your license. I strongly suggest you get all of them except perhaps the passenger endorsement, unless you want to drive a bus. There are Class A, B, and C type licenses. We are only interested in Class A. That means you can also drive the same vehicles for which a Class B or C is required.

If all you want to do is drive a bus, I think all you need is a Class B license with the passenger endorsement. I have no interest in riding on a bus at all and certainly am never going to want to drive one. That is up to you to decide.

By all means expand your horizons and increase your potential job opportunities by getting your doubles/triples endorsement, tanker endorsement, and hazmat endorsement. Just recently hazmat also started requiring finger prints and some other minor items. I did not have to go through that in my most recent license renewal as I met the deadline by a couple weeks, so once again I would suggest checking with your state licensing authority to get the specifics. They can tell you all about any requirements and you do not have to pay for such information.

While I have all of these endorsements, other than hauling hazardous materials on a few occasions, I have never made use of any of the others. In other words I claim no involvement whatsoever with tankers or double and triple trailers. That is a specialty area, personal preference, and beyond the scope of this book. I have seen them going down the highway and I have also seen them off the highway in various states of destruction.

While I am sure some drivers love it and probably get paid an extra penny or two for the privilege, I have no interest in finding out what it is like to pull three trailers behind me. I can barely see all the way to the back of one fifty-three footer, let alone try to see a block back down the highway to make sure all my extra parts remain attached. No thank you. I will pass on that opportunity.

Additionally, I watched CNN where some lucky videographer had captured a fuel tanker in full explosion. It was one massive ball of flames and I bet it was damn well warm in there. Needless to say, the driver did not survive. I'm not interested in these experiences either. There are far more interesting ways to go trucking. Thanks anyway. However, in the event that somewhere down the road you come upon a high paying opportunity to operate one of these units, you will only have invested the little time it took to pass the endorsement tests. It doesn't cost any extra.

Once you have passed all the written tests and possibly taken a DOT (Department of Transportation) physical, which apparently anyone can pass, you will be able to obtain your learner's permit. You will eventually have to pass the physical before you are allowed to operate out on the highway, but you do want your new company to pay for it. Make sure that they do.

The physical is amazing to me in that so many of the drivers you see around the country are anything but fit. Some drivers are so massively overweight they can barely get in and out of the cab of their trucks. And yet in order for them to legally operate a commercial vehicle, they had to have passed a similar test to the ones I have had to take.

I always seem to have a relatively high blood pressure reading. I imagine this is partially due to the fact that I usually consume a bit of coffee prior to my test. Either way, I have always managed to pass. It is rather unusual to me though, being in reasonably good condition, that others I would consider to be incredibly out of shape have also passed. So I must guess that the requirements are not really that stringent.

There is nothing really complicated about the examination. They pretty much take your blood pressure and say "Turn your head and cough." Except in the case of a woman, perhaps they are only told to turn their head. Not sure how that one goes, having never witnessed the female DOT exam. Have yet to receive my first invitation to the party.

You will also receive a vision test, so unless you have previously memorized the vision charts that they use, you will be required to see. It's hard to believe that they actually expect potential big rig drivers to be able to see the road in front of them. Seriously though, you will also have to pass a small hearing exam, so they actually expect you to be able to hear. Considering all the loud music I have been involved with over the years, I also have managed to get by that exam without any complications. Truly amazing!

Once you have obtained the learner's permit you are ready to proceed onward. Lucky you. At that time you will either visit the local truck driver school or you will be affiliating with one of the many companies that will basically take a bum off the street and make him a truck driver. Pay attention here!! All truck schools and truck companies are **NOT** the same. Let's do it again. All truck schools and truck companies are **NOT** the same. You must take the time to shop around or you may regret it.

At truck driving school you will learn exactly what it takes to actually obtain your Class A CDL. At any particular company you will also learn exactly what it takes to obtain your Class A CDL. Once you have the license you **do not** know how to drive yet. You do not want to be lured into any false sense of security by thinking, that just because you have the license, you know what you are doing. That will take a bit of time and lots of practice.

I won't tell you that by either going with a trucking company or going through a truck driver training school you will be better off. Different situations require different solutions. I considered both.

Make no mistake, most of these schools and companies are charging you big time for their services and the variation in pricing is sometimes ludicrous to say the least. Unless you have a veritable warehouse of cash, be willing plead poverty. Definitely you must shop around.

If you don't ask, you will not receive. Try to get it for less. As in real estate, EVERYTHING is negotiable. If they tell you otherwise, be willing to walk away. However always leave your options open. Tell them, "it costs way too much, but I will think it over and after speaking with some of your competitors, I'll let you know." The fact is most of these trucking companies will also pay you back for what they are charging for their "professional driver training."

These trucking companies will all "learn you real good how to drive them big rigs," as long as you will commit to drive for them for a specified period of time. A truck driving school can be a better choice because it gives you more options. I am big on options, which is why for me the private truck driving school was my choice. After you have your license, you have the option of going to one of any number of truck companies, rather than being tied to that one company that sounded so good on the phone. They all try to impress you on the phone with all the great things their company has to offer, but it ain't always as they say. Take that to the bank.

Like I said, most of them are charging for their services, and most companies will reimburse you for some or all of the money you spent at truck school. For example, for each month you drive for ABC Trucking, that company will reimburse you $150 to pay off your trucking school obligation. Just make sure they do. Getting it in writing would not be a bad idea. You probably won't have any problem with reimbursement. I didn't. But you never know. Trucking companies are well known for having selective memories when it comes time for reimbursements (not only truck school tuition / if you are owed anything, always write it down and always watch your check to make sure you are paid back what you are owed).

Once again not all truck companies or driving schools are created equal. For example, the school I went through in Colorado was for me a tremendous experience. My school was a lesser known school than some of the big names you see around the country. It also cost substantially less.

There are literally thousands of sites on the Internet, that will allow you to explore numerous options for companies or truck schools. The yellow pages of your local phone directory can put you in touch with a company right up the street from you. Stop by your local truck stop and pick up a small library of free publications promoting numerous trucking firms as the most incredible step you will ever take in your life on the road. They will all tell you why they are the best, will pay you the most, are the most family oriented companies out there, and many other lines of absolute nonsense that are intended to compel you to make that call to their ever present recruiting staff. "Yes indeed, we are available 24 hours a day and hoping to entice you into that brand new KW." Always remain skeptical.

No matter how you go about it, you will need to speak either on the phone or in person with several of these businesses in order to make an informed decision on how you will be spending your future life in trucking. Do not accept what any of these fine folks tell you as the Gospel. Chances are more than good that you are at least in part being fed a line of garbage.

Once they get you to their facility, reality can become a nightmare of astronomical proportions. You are then subject to their way of doing business, and are more likely out of necessity to be agreeable to things you might have thought intolerable last week, when you were back home a thousand miles from where you are now. You need to learn in advance what to expect from several of these businesses. Nothing can be 100% (except my guarantee to "tell it like it is"), so you need to increase your odds of success by asking numerous companies, numerous questions.

You can pay them up front or you can sign your life away for a little while and finance your tuition. They will generally finance anyone. They will finance you because you have collateral. In financing a real estate purchase, they have your home as collateral. In this case you will probably agree to go drive for ABC Trucking, who just happens to have connections with your truck school. Their collateral is your ability to produce income for the trucking company. Therefore, on top of your massive earnings equated to your cents per mile driven, ABC Trucking is also going to supply you with that $150/month that you need to pay off your truck school loan.

This can be good or bad. It is good, because as I stated before you can be a bum off the street and all of a sudden you have a rent free place to live, a legitimate job that pays reasonably well, a way to save a rather substantial amount of cash in a relatively short period of time, and you are always on vacation going to various exciting parts of the country (all company paid).

It can be bad in that you are now tied to that one

company for an extended period of time. You are obligated to pay for truck school, whether you received your training from the private trucking school or from an immediate affiliation with a specific company that trained you. You are also obligated to repay your debt in the event that they fire you for crashing one of their trucks into a school bus full of kids, or falling asleep at the wheel and driving your brand new hundred thousand dollar Freightliner over the side of a snowy mountain cliff.

If on the other hand you paid up front for your truck school as I did, you always have the option of walking away from that which you find unacceptable. As I said, I like having options. Now having said that, I will tell you just what I learned when starting out. It is very important that you really try and spend your first year or so with one company. You not only get a real chance to learn to drive. You also establish a bit of credibility within the trucking industry.

Then you can go shopping for something else armed with an important weapon. Experience! You can say, "I have a full year of OTR driving experience with ABC Trucking." That says something to the other companies out there (who by the way are anxiously waiting to scarf up your services with all kinds of lies and frivolous banter about the great things that XYZ Trucking will provide to you).

There are always trade offs and the grass always looks greener somewhere else. It may be, and you will never know for sure until you jump. But, all this makes it very important for you to make the best choice in picking a school or company. The school I went to cost less and living accommodations for the few weeks I attended included residing at the house of the guy who ran the school. Not only that, but I had my own private bedroom, all of our dinners were cooked by the head of the school (I swear this guy was a gourmet chef), big screen TV and rental movies every night, and we had our own vehicle to transport us back and forth to truck school every day.

On the Fourth of July, we had the day off and went to a big party at one of the instructor's houses. All in all my truck driving school experience was quite satisfactory. At the end of my two or three weeks of classroom and actual driver training, I took my driving test, (administered by the head of the school and gourmet chef), got my actual Class A CDL with all the endorsements, and went off to drive for a company which was in fact affiliated with my driving school.

Your experience will be different, but it is going to be what you make out of it. Get on the Internet, do a Google search of truck jobs, truck schools, and anything else you can think of in your area or even in any area you might be interested in relocating to. What? You don't have an Internet connection? Go to almost any local library. It is free. I am even bigger on free than I am on options.

Once you have established a list of schools, a list of potential trucking companies, and a long list of questions you want answered, pick up the phone and call. What? You don't have a phone either? Guess what? Most of these places have toll free numbers with people on the other end that are just dying to answer all of your questions. Pay phones are everywhere and amazingly provide free access to toll free connections.

After you have spoken with a few of these folks and seriously checked out their websites to see what they are potentially offering, you will become a bit more familiar with what to expect. Something I have always done is ask questions to which I already know the answer. You will be surprised to find out who is lying to you and you will receive invaluable reinforcement in regard to the new things you are learning with an accurate response from a recruiter, that may be telling you the truth.

Do not be afraid to ask anything you want an answer to, as they need you much more than you need them. You also are making a lifestyle change. Make sure you know what you need to know. Before jumping in, be sure there is water in the pool.

There are very few things that will keep these companies from hiring you. If you have a DUI or some other such negativity attached to your driving record, it better have been a long time ago. Oddly enough there are a few companies that will even overlook this.

Several years back and mostly out of curiosity, I went to a driver recruitment meeting held by one of the bigger and well known companies at a local hotel. The recruiter basically said to the group of attendees, "We will hire anyone unless they are on parole or probation." The guy sitting next to me stood up and said, "Well, uh guess that let's me out..." As he was walking out the door, the recruiter said to him, "Be sure and check back when you get off probation. We've got a driving job waiting for you."

In spite of this recruiter's optimism, I will say this. If your driving record is filled with bad news, if you are on parole, or if you are prone to crashing your vehicles, you may wish to reconsider your options. I for one do not look forward to running in to you on the highway.

One other thing not to do is to over analyze these companies. Most of them are very similar and all have positives and negatives. By thorough and proper questioning you will get most of the answers you need. You want to know important things such as:

-Are you going to fully reimburse me for everything I spent at LMN Truck Driving School?

-How long do I have to spend on the road with one of your "professional trainers" until I get my own truck?

-If I hate my trainer can I get another one or have authorization to break his legs? (You may not want to ask that one; even though it is something you will probably think about.)

-Do we get paid for orientation?

-How much am I being paid during my training period?

-Are we paid on a per diem basis? (means more money in your check and good if you don't itemize your taxes/ also MORE beneficial to the employer, because they pay less employment taxes on your income, but they aren't likely to tell you that)

-Are your trucks speed governed? At what speed? (As a new driver, slower is probably better. Just stay out of the fast lane or you will anger the drivers with the faster trucks.)

-Can I bring my Rottweilers? (Many companies allow smaller dogs or cats, with some kind of pet deposit, in case your little puppy has a taste for fine upholstery. But, you may want to think real hard about whom you are sharing your small living area with.)

-Do you use Qualcoms? (satellite communication system in reality used so your company always knows where their trucks are and to make sure you aren't going 50 miles out of route to visit your mother or your girl friend, without their permission)

-Do they have no slip seating? (This is some more of that high level trucker terminology. It means that when you take a few days off, do you return to your same truck, or are you going to get a surprise and be stuck with some other driver's problems and filth? When you return from your relaxing time off, you may be stuck with some cigarette smoke filled antique, that someone else was dying to get out of before the transmission fell apart. A nice thing about returning to your same vehicle is that you are much more likely to know of any potential upcoming mechanical disasters, and much less likely to lie down on a vermin filled mattress left by a previous mutant buffoon driver, who rarely made use of his frequent fueler card and the free showers at the truck stop.

-Are they going to bug me about idling my engine too long? (Important stuff as many companies will dog you to death in regard to it. They expect you to shut it off whether you need air conditioning for the 100 degree heat or heat for the -10 degree cold.)

-If you are not already in the same town, "What kind of transportation are you offering to get to your facility?" (I have done everything from driving there myself, to receiving a cab ride to the airport and a first class plane ticket to the destination terminal.)

Trust me, you can learn a good deal about what a company really thinks about its drivers by the way they transport you to their facility, and the hotel they put you up in for your company orientation. Make no mistake about it, while it may be necessary, riding a bus for 16 hours stinks, and if that is all you are being offered, perhaps you need to reexamine your "options." Let me say, that I have never ridden a bus to any trucking facility, and I NEVER will.

There are many questions you need to ask and get substantial answers to. Write up your own list of the things that are important to you. However, I repeat. Do not over analyze here. No companies are going to be exactly what you want and some are even downright pathetic. There are so many companies out there literally begging for drivers, that if you don't like what you hear, tell them you will think about it (leaving your options open of course) and move on to another. The more time you spend talking with representatives of several trucking companies and several different truck driving schools, the more you will learn about what you can expect from them and their facility.

You will be able to figure it all out with a bit of research. None of them are perfect, but if you have to the best of your abilities checked them out thoroughly, you are likely to be the most content with your final decision. Most trucking companies haul freight and they are very similar in their operations. Most truck driving schools are going to get you through their program and get you that all important Commercial Driver's License.

That said, let me emphasize that the best trucking jobs have nothing at all to do with hauling freight. Unfortunately you are not likely to obtain one of those coveted positions without putting in a bit of time dragging trailers full of groceries about the country. We'll discuss this unusual option later on and in much greater detail. That I promise.

At this point it is like standing on the high diving board at the local pool. Have you ever stood on the high diving board? From ground level it doesn't look too bad, but when you actually climb the ladder, walk out to the end and look down at the water, it can be intimidating if not terrifying to be up that high. As long as you can see the water, you will probably survive it. Jump!!

<u>Getting Started</u>

3. Learning How To Drive, Or I Want To Kill My Trainer

Assuming you passed your actual driving test, obtained your CDL and have picked the company for which you will drive for the next year or so, you now move forward to the orientation and training process. For the next two or three days you will most likely sit in a room with several or even many other drivers and learn about your new company. The excitement here is almost unbearable. Hang in there. This is the easy part. They do try and make you comfortable in your new environment.

It is very likely that a good percentage of the other drivers there already have substantial experience with other companies. Why? Because in the transportation industry, driver turnover is tremendous. The vast majority of drivers do not stay long with the same company.

The fact is that there are so many things for a driver to get annoyed about with most companies, and so many companies looking to attract new drivers, that it becomes relatively easy to job hop in the transportation industry. Companies spend a substantial part of their revenue replacing drivers that move on and yet in my experience they are generally clueless when it comes to discerning the causes of their lack of success in the department of driver retention. They very often lose drivers because of their own ignorance and lack of addressing some of the most obvious and common problems that are prevalent in the industry.

This is not for a new driver to concern themselves with yet, as you are here to learn to drive, not look for another company. You have made your choice. Now stick with it. Your training will be the hardest thing you will ever have to deal with in the trucking biz, unless you are forced to traverse Flatbush Avenue in Brooklyn. That's another parable for later on.

You will probably spend the next few nights at one of the local motels. Here again you can learn about your company. If they have stuck you in the local flop house full of what appear to be bums and people on some sort of prison release program, chances are good this company thinks little of its drivers. Watch out now and be prepared for further surprises down the road apiece! It will eventually come to pass just as sure as that old burrito from the convenience store that you had to stop at.

If on the other hand you are placed in a quality establishment with a private room in a better part of town, and with numerous amenities, take note of that also. It does mean something. As an initial company gesture, they are showing you that you are an important part of the future of their company and they are saying, "Welcome to ABC Trucking, we respect you and your decision to become a part of our success." The fact that you are now being well cared for does not preclude the potential that somewhere down the road you may well grow to despise this company, and memories of your experiences there may be far less than satisfactory.

Companies that try to stick you in a room you will share with some other potential driver, that you have never met before, are being cheap. I do not do the roommate situation and you should not either. A company that expects you to share living accommodations with some potentially scroungy character that you have never met and know absolutely nothing about is definitely showing you their true colors. If this is a concern for you, it may be one of those things to put on your pre-employment questionnaire check list.

Too often truck drivers have a tendency to be unkempt, unwashed, foul smelling characters of questionable repute. If you think I'm kidding, just take a walk through your local truck stop some time. The mutants run rampant. It can truly be an eye opening experience. So, I say "No roommates, thank you."

So now you are at your first day of orientation. Most of your time will be spent filling out numerous papers and forms, but in reality one of the very first things you will be doing is going to the local clinic for the DOT physical (if you have not already done so, and if the company requires a new one) and most importantly a urine test (drug screen). If you do not pass your urine test, chances are good that you won't get that first class plane ride home. If you are concerned about your ability to pass, you may wish to make other arrangements for your future.

If you started out with twenty people in your original orientation group, do not be surprised if you gradually notice that number diminish over the next few days. Recruiters work so hard and fast to get drivers to that orientation that sometimes they fail to notice that one of their drivers was fired for beating his previous dispatcher into a coma, someone else is wanted for armed robbery, someone else failed to pass their physical, and of course there are a few that fail the urine test.

These undesirable folks will magically disappear from your orientation and when you get back to the hotel you will be saying, "I wonder what happened to that guy from Portland." You will most likely never see these people again. They are quickly removed from the group, so as to not affect that positive morale and high energy level your new company is attempting to instill in you and the remaining drivers.

If you are a brand new driver they may still want to give you the standard company driving test to see what you are capable of doing. It usually consists of 10 or 20 minutes of driving around the area. That should give you no problem as a newly licensed professional.

However, they are probably going to make you try and back in to some nice tight parking space big enough for a mini bike. They do not really expect much from you as a new driver, but that will not stop you from not wanting to embarrass yourself.

Make no mistake about it. Backing up a tractor trailer is the hardest single thing a driver will have to do. Once you have mastered the art of backing, you will be set. This will not happen overnight, so do not be frustrated when your nerves get the best of you and you manage to screw up your backing test. It will take a lot of practice, but you will eventually get it down.

With your tests out of the way, you will most likely watch some of the finest films ever made, on the subject of safe driving. These are true classics of the genre and the excitement is almost beyond belief. They are also guaranteed as a cure for sleep deprivation. You will probably also be blessed with listening to various people from your company as they let you know how certain things are done at ABC Trucking.

Always be careful what papers they have you sign. They probably aren't doing anything outrageous, but be sure you read carefully. I had one company later claim that I had abandoned their truck, when I had actually left it at the very terminal where I started from, where I actually parked my personal vehicle, and where I had in fact previously agreed in writing to leave the vehicle upon my departure.

This all came back to a paper from my orientation, which I told them I could not agree with. I crossed out what they had written and inserted my intent, that if I was to leave the company, that rather than returning my truck to the terminal they wanted it at, I would return it to the terminal out of which I was based, and where I had parked my car. They agreed to that at the time, but apparently forgot our agreement, when I decided it was the appropriate moment for my departure.

Make sure you get agreements you can live with at the start and get signed copies for your records. Above all else, prepare in advance for something that has a very real potential to become reality. These companies are big on trying to nail you early with things they have had to deal with frequently. They know what to expect in advance, things that you are not even remotely thinking about. For them it may be self preservation. For a driver it is nothing but a screw job down the road. So on this subject I say pay close attention to all documents that they require you to sign, such that they do not return later to haunt you.

At some point in the process they will introduce you to your new trainer. This is a person who will be responsible for teaching you how to drive. Up to this point you have only been taught how to get your Class A CDL. You are not yet a driver as you will find out. You will most likely spend the next several weeks or more, 24 hours a day with this person. Compatibility is of the essence here, because more than likely you will be approaching insanity by the end of your training period. If your trainer smokes and you do not, this can be a problem.

I am convinced that most drivers smoke. Nearly every

driver I see pulling into a truck stop has a cigarette sticking out of his left hand. When you go into the restaurant at the truck stop, there is nearly always a section reserved for professional drivers. They always have the cable TV set up and ash trays on every table. As someone who does not find it necessary to have my daily dose of tar and nicotine, I always avoid this section. The non-smoker section is usually way in the back, where there are no waitresses and no cable TV. Sounds to me like non-smoker discrimination. Oh, well. Not everything is as it should be.

Back to the point though, if you smoke, you want a smoking trainer. If you don't smoke, being in a truck with a smoker can be instant incompatibility. Trust me. My very first assigned trainer was a smoker and he wisely asked me if I smoked. I wasn't really concerned at the time, but I am certain that it would have been a problem down the road. I was switched to another trainer.

As it turned out, I did run into this guy several times over the next few years and he actually ended up being a friend. Prior to driving, this guy had been an assistant pathologist. You would be surprised at the varying background of a lot of truck drivers. As I have said not all big rig operators are beset with the genes of a mutant buffoon.

Returning to the compatibility issue, you are in fact going to be in very close quarters with your trainer for an extended period at 24 hours a day, so you really have to try and get along. You also have to realize that it is your trainer, who is responsible for releasing you to obtain your own truck. And let me emphasize that the feeling of being done with your trainer and getting into your own rig is almost overwhelming ecstasy.

I learned fast that I could never be a team driver. It drove me crazy being crammed into that small living space with another person who I barely knew. On top of that, trying to sleep when someone else is driving is a virtual impossibility for me. Whenever the truck went around a corner, I would wake up instantly with thoughts of going off a cliff. That feeling has never diminished.

In my case I was lucky though. I had the opportunity to work with three separate trainers under very different circumstances and for a comparatively short time to most other rookie drivers. For that I thank the old lucky stars, because it did get a bit tense on occasion.

My first company, which is no longer in operation, was owned by the same guy who owned the Colorado Rockies Baseball team. Thus and oddly enough the trainer trucks were fancy new Freightliners emblazoned with the logo of the Rockies. Right away you were a celebrity of the trucking industry by driving around in these rigs.

My first trainer was a very helpful and informative fellow. Several people in the company told me that he was the best trainer they had and I was lucky to get him. I'm not sure if this was the truth or if they just wanted me to feel special. It is of no consequence as all that mattered is that he was a wealth of information on how to drive 18 wheelers. To this day I am still reminded of certain things he would repeat over and over for my benefit. It is important to hear certain things over and over. After awhile it becomes a part of your routine. You do it, but you don't really have to think about it. It just happens, and how fortunate one is to be endowed with a good memory. It can be a life saver.

I actually spent no more than a couple weeks with this guy. We went back and forth across the country for a week or so, from Denver to Baltimore and back out to California. When we arrived in Fontana, California, I was told that my trainer was going to take some time off at home. So, I spent the next week hanging out at a local motel and at the company's expense. I think that in that week I forgot damn near everything I had previously learned. It is important when you are starting out to keep going. The more you do it, the better you get. That applies to many endeavors. Doesn't it?

My trainer, and we'll call him Jack (in case his wife reads this), was involved in marital complications. His wife wanted him off the road and I can't say that I blame her. While we were traveling from Baltimore back to California, we conveniently stopped in St. Louis so my trainer, Jack, had the opportunity to spend the night with his girl friend (she was someone he had previously trained with the company). Such things can come up in the world of truck driving. You just never know.

Anyway, when my trainer, Jack, eventually returned from his week off, he had in fact decided to give up training and actually only stayed with the company another week or two. So needless to say I was out a good trainer. When we returned to Denver, there were no OTR trainers available, so the company put me back in the local motel and proceeded to send me out daily for training with one of the local drivers. This was great. I didn't have to be locked up in a small cab 24 hours a day with someone I hardly knew, and I was still getting plenty of driving practice. This was the way to learn to drive for me.

Now after a couple weeks of actually driving, my confidence level was soaring. I'm thinking, "Hell yes, I've got this down like a xxxxxx xxxxxx." I was beginning to wonder if it was time for me to have my own ride. Surprise! Surprise!! Trainer number three showed up.

I was less than excited about hitting the road with someone else I didn't know. This was a very stressful time.

Here I am thinking I was getting pretty good at this trucker stuff, and here the company was getting ready to send me out again with another trainer. I was not real happy at this new prospect.

Here is where options can come in. I seriously thought about heading out. My Corvette was still sitting at the local Corvette dealer on consignment and all I had to do was go back, pick it up, and drive off into the sunset. I was ready to say bye bye to trucking. But I didn't. I decided that I have come this far and I will continue on. And that was that.

I hit the road with my new trainer and I was maybe 45 minutes outside of Denver when this guy started talking about alternative lifestyles. Now as an accomplished guitarist of many years, I knew all about alternative music (and never thought much of it). However, it took me a few more minutes before I realized my new trainer was not espousing the virtues of the music industry. He was talking about being gay. He was and I am not. Over the next few days I began to realize that this guy was very different from me. He spent an inordinate amount of time on the phone and had some of the weirdest conversations I have ever heard.

When you are on the road in such close proximity to another person you tend to learn plenty about them. I spent about a week on the road with my third trainer and boy did I learn all about "alternative lifestyles."

On two separate occasions (once in Louisville, Kentucky and once at a truck stop in South Carolina), my illustrious trainer came to me and said, "You can do whatever you want, but don't move the truck." He then proceeded to get into a car with some guy, that he had apparently just met, and disappear for the night. Twice he did this and it was just strange to me. However, I did not complain, because it got my team driver out of the truck.

I will say that in spite of his strange behaviors and "alternative lifestyle," this guy was extremely knowledgeable on trucking and about a lot of other stuff too. As we were driving through either North or South Carolina, he pointed to a large empty grass filled field and mentioned that John Wayne had filmed "The Horse Soldiers" right there. I was impressed. I don't know if it was true, but this guy acted as if he knew everything about everything. So I did not question it.

Something else this guy told me always sticks with me. It is something that **could happen to any driver at any time** and it is definitely worthy of mention. One night a few years back, he was cruisin' down the road in his big truck, when he noticed a car coming right at him, head on, and in his lane. What do you do? You only have a few seconds to make a decision and take appropriate action.

You could swerve off the road to avoid a collision. In this case you would probably wreck and at least you would cause damage to your rig and maybe yourself. In that event you can probably guess that the other driver would keep right on going, and after the state patrol officer listened carefully to your logical explanation of why you ran into a tree, he would likely write **YOU** a ticket for reckless driving. So I ask again, what do you do with only a few quick seconds to react?

I can't disagree with what trainer #3 did, even though the results were tragic. He maintained his lane, slowed down and let this driver hit him head on. The driver was legally drunk and was killed in the accident. No loss there.

Unfortunately, his wife and two kids were also in the car and were also killed. Certainly this was not a desirable result and yet he did what he felt he should with only seconds to react. A big truck is not a Corvette and you can't just dodge around a head on collision.

I asked him if it bothers him knowing he had killed those four people. He said it does and yet he can live with it. He was not found to be at fault in any way. Most assuredly this is something to ponder as you travel about the country. It can happen to anyone at any time.

After being on the road and dealing with a week of trainer #3 and his "alternative lifestyle" we got back to Denver. I had truly had all I wanted from my week with #3. While I had learned plenty, I had no interest in continuing on with this guy. In other words, I was definitely at the point of saying bye bye to trucking again. I walked into the office where three or four of the terminal management guys were sitting around. At this point I received a collective laugh from them.

The head guy looked at me and said, "If you could put up with that, you could put up with anything." They knew that #3 was a bit different. I told them I did think he was a nice guy and very informative. He had actually showed me a picture of his ex wife. They proceeded to tell me that he had in fact been married, but that the picture was not of a woman. I had to admit that she wasn't all that attractive, but I did not realize that his wife was a man.

The moral of the story here is that it is not so important who is training you, but the fact that they are good at what they are doing. Fortunately for me, #3 gave the company the go ahead for me to get into my own truck. Thus ended my experience of being trained in the life of big rig driving.

Looking back on my only three weeks of actual driver training, I knew inside that I was ready to go on my own. I could not take any more training and I knew then, that I could NEVER EVER be a team driver. Just for the record, three weeks is just not enough training time for most people.

Twice that long is not enough, but that is most likely all you will get from most companies. They want a revenue producer, not a driving student.

It will take you longer than a few weeks on the road to really be a confident and safe driver. Even though you may think you have it down, you can never take your mind off what you are doing. It could actually take several years of OTR action before you have really seen the majority of potential disasters that may come your way. There is always something you can do to improve your skill as a safe and competent operator, and the longer you drive, your potential for improvement increases.

That is not to say that someone who has been driving for many years is not going to be struck by a moment of ignorance. Just because you have been out there since the beginning of time doesn't necessarily make you a candidate for the Nobel Prize for Professional Truck Drivers. Certainly you are aware of that lofty award for the best and the brightest on the highway given each year. Ok, I am kidding again.

It is very possible if not even likely that a very experienced driver may take for granted his masterful skill in operating big trucks under any circumstances, and not be paying any attention to what he is doing. I am certain that it occurs daily and with precision. It only takes a second of inattentiveness to cause death and destruction that will haunt you to your grave.

Not all trucking accidents are caused by new drivers just out of truck school. In fact the opposite is often the case. A new driver is most likely to try and be overly cautious. The trick is to always maintain vigilance on the highway. No matter how good you may think you are, there is always going to be that minivan dude that is inevitably hiding in your blind spot and begging you to run him over.

Too often people in their cars do the most incredibly moronic things, when in the presence of 80,000 pounds of potential annihilation. They would be fully deserving of being crushed and tossed into the scrap heap at the junk yard and yet, you do not want that on your conscience.

When you are behind the wheel of your big truck, you need to always be aware of everything that is going on around you. Even when you think you are completely alone on the highway, with no one around for twenty miles, that is the time to be most aware. Inevitably Mr. Minivan driver will be right along side of you on the road, having come from absolutely nowhere, and anxiously awaiting his more than deserved fate.

The key to this awareness is proper training. It is not something a trainer can teach you. You must drill it into your "innate driver sensory awareness system," such that it becomes more than second nature. You must train yourself, because you and only you are legally and morally responsible for any and all choices you make as you travel down the road. You don't ever want to mess up if it can be avoided. Always pay attention and always be aware.

If you can pull this off, you will not be paranoid of running over and squashing Mr. Minivan driver. Without even thinking about it, you will just know to always be watching your mirrors, but not always entirely trusting those mirrors. As you are waiting in anticipation of that inevitable surprise, when it comes you won't be off guard, because you were expecting it all along. You were prepared as always for the inevitable.

Anyway, I was in fact now on my own with my own

company truck. Yup, on my own. Hell yeah!! I got to pick from 5 or 6 trucks sitting on the terminal lot. So I picked out a nice old Freightliner with just over 500k miles and off I went. Free at last! Free at last! I was absolutely thrilled to be on my own. Free at last!!

The Author with the truck school staff and another driving student.

This is the Author with another typical truck driving student alongside of the first truck I ever drove.

The Author with my very first company truck & Ellis.

My second truck is on the right & my actual Colorado Rockies training truck is on the left.

On The Road Again

On The Road Again

1. Now You're In Charge. Don't Mess Up.

As a new driver I said to myself, "Certainly, they will give me something nice and easy to start out." NOT!! My very first trip on my own as a solo company driver of 80,000 lbs of bone crushing, flesh mauling metal was a meat load going into New York City! NOBODY WANTS TO DRIVE IN NEW YORK CITY!!

How could they do this to me on my very first load? What could possibly be worse for a beginner driver than to be sent into New York City? Everyone hears the horrible stories of drivers being robbed and killed while driving around the biggest baddest city in the United States. How could they possibly do this to me? Drivers in New York City are all crazy. I am screwed and I am doomed!

However, I grew up and learned to drive in Connecticut, which is just a few minutes from New York City. Knowing the area pretty well, I figured I can pull this off. When I was nineteen years old, I jumped into my old 1969 Z-28 Camaro and drove non-stop 1867 miles from Littleton, Colorado to Stamford, Connecticut. Having just lived there the year before, I was excited to return to the old stomping ground and hang out with the old friends. Thus I figured, I've done this before and I can do it again. The only difference is that what I'm driving is about 71 feet long and it weighs damn near 80,000 lbs. It was intimidating at best.

The only real difference in driving around in the northeast quarter of the United States is that you better be carrying a substantial bank roll. Heading east and once you get to Illinois, there are non-stop tolls. Indiana, Ohio, Pennsylvania, New Jersey, and on into New York you will be greeted with those happy little signs announcing another toll booth. They are endless, seeming to appear about every couple miles, and sucking the dollars out of your wallet faster than a blackjack dealer in Reno.

The bridge tolls in New York are unbelievable. They were $30 a pop the last time I passed through and on top of that you can sometimes sit in traffic for hours just waiting to go that last mile or so to the toll booth. There is little doubt why drivers like to avoid the northeast. There are often ways around some of the tolls and traffic jams, but sometimes the distance you have to drive makes no sense. So, you either deal with it, or as I very often do, drive through in the middle of the night and avoid much of the potential for disaster.

As this was my very first solo trip, I really wanted everything to go well and I definitely wanted to be on time. Pretty much driving non-stop from Denver, I got into NYC on a Sunday evening for a Monday AM delivery, so traffic was not too bad.

I got the directions on my Qualcom (satellite communication system used by many companies). It was certainly a time of tension, knowing that if you made even one wrong turn, you could be on the road to nowhere. The potential to end up lost and screwed, impossibly trying to turn around your seventy one feet of tractor trailer in some neighborhood you have no business in was very real. You did not want to be facing that feeling of knowing you'd better get out of here fast, if you want to avoid any impending pitfalls or an untimely demise. This was not the time to make a mistake.

I followed those directions exactly, finding myself at the Nebraska Land meat warehouse in the Bronx. They let me park over night on their lot, unloaded me in the morning, and I was off without a hitch. Needless to say I was pleased all to hell to be done with my very first load and out of New York City.

Amazingly, I was not attacked by a band of crazed drug addicts, no one broke into the back of the trailer to steal my very valuable meat load, nor did I drive over the side of the George Washington Bridge crashing headlong into the massive Hudson River. It was smooth all the way. The intimidation factor is ever present when you are in a place the size of NYC, so you must maintain an ever present vigilance and be prepared for all possible eventualities.

What I did do, in spite of my nervousness, trepidation, and sheer terror was get my first glimpse of the best reason for driving a big truck (other than getting paid). When you first go over the GW Bridge, you get a glimpse of the skyline of the most impressive city on the planet. You are now a "professional tourist."

I would never suggest that anyone live in NYC, but visiting and just seeing it is incredible. Growing up just a short distance away in Connecticut, I took the train many times into New York. But, to this day, and while I have driven a big rig through the streets of NYC on several occasions, I have never driven there in a car, and I do not intend to.

This however was an exhilarating experience. New York City is definitely one of the sights to see. Don't miss it. Even if you only do it once it will be worthwhile. After you have done it you may say to yourself, "I don't believe I just did NYC." Just do it! Let's see. How's that song go about "New York, New York?" "If I can drive a big rig there, I can drive it anywhere." Oh well, something like that, huh?

Just remember that, unless you are with one of those companies that has a half dozen or so toll tags, that allow you to drive right on through all the toll booths, you better be prepared to carry a couple hundred extra dollars. At thirty and some even over forty dollars a pop, your money goes very fast.

I actually drove for one of those toll tag companies for a short time and do not recommend them (no company names, sorry). That is something you will have to figure out on your own. More about NYC later. At this point I am exhausted just thinking about it.

A shot of the New York City skyline, Empire State
Building included, from the cab of my truck, while
actually driving over the Hudson River, across the
George Washington Bridge, and living to tell about it.

A shot from I-70 going through Saint Louis, and yes it is
also truck in motion and camera in hand. Drivin' &
shootin'!

Cruisin' over Hoover Dam was an experience. Since 9/11 no big rigs allowed and for obvious reasons.

Hangin' out behind Six Flags Amusement Park in Atlanta just for fun.

On the Road Again

2. More Miles, More Money, So keep On Rollin'

Whenever I make my "escape," as I will refer to it, from a large metropolitan area (ex. New York, Los Angeles, Chicago), I have a tendency to drive a long way. It is just kind of relaxing to know that you have in fact made it out alive and free of the ten thousand obstacles that got in your way each and every time you visited.

Although you are going to see most of the best scenery in the daylight, you can often make the best time at night. So if I have just spent a long day delivering and then picking up a new load in the middle of the big city, I may just keep rolling until I am far far away from it all. In the middle of the night, the majority of cars are off the road, the greater percentage of big rigs are parked at the truck stops and rest areas, and the highway is all yours. Hopefully.

To make it much clearer, if you are in one of those slow company trucks, you are going to make much better time by driving when you are not spending thirty minutes or more at a pop just trying to get around Gomer Vacationer. Gomer is in his big ole Winnebago, with another trailer attached to the back of it, and then a car attached to the back of that trailer (pulling doubles).

You will often find that you can't quite get around him, and every time you try, magically twenty more cars and ten big rigs want to get around you first. The irritation level is unbelievable. No matter what you do you are stuck behind this guy.

Finally you get your chance to go. You pull out into the hammer lane and let it rip. Unfortunately Gomer Vacationer somehow then decides he is tired of everyone passing him, and so he speeds up just enough so that your speed governor, set at 65 miles per hour, will not quite let you get by. Irritation deluxe.

If only you had missiles attached to the front of your truck and could just blow this guy out of the way. But alas no. Of course, as soon as you give up and pull back behind Gomer again, he decides to slow back down. This same process will repeat several times, until you think you can't take it any more.

Yes indeed, you must follow him to the end of the earth, or until he has to stop for gas. Sooner or later he will get off the highway, won't he? And then when he finally hits that exit ramp to the rest area the relief is overwhelming. "Hell yes!!" Finally it happened.

This is why you might consider covering ground at night. There are other reasons for driving at night and we will go through all of them eventually. If there is something I really want to see in the daylight I will, but the benefits of driving those extra miles to get through a big city at 3 in the morning and avoiding the two hour traffic jam that will inevitably greet you in the AM far outweigh the negatives.

I will confess to occasionally driving many more miles than I am supposed to and yet I rarely drive when I start to get tired. Drivers fall asleep at the wheel every day. You do not want that to happen to you. You may never wake up. If you are tired, you get off the highway fast.

Even a quick nap can be the difference between life, and crashing into a concrete retaining wall at 65 mph and burning to death, crushed in the cab of your truck. I do not make this stuff up. I've seen the results of careless driving again and again. Many folks come to a very uncomfortable end every day on the highway.

I like to drive until the sun is about to come up and then pull over for a bit of sleep at a truck stop or local rest area. This is pretty much backwards to what the average driver will do. When I wake up, I frequently am the only truck left in the parking area. It feels funny, until I realize that I am actually hundreds of miles ahead of where I would be had I followed the rest of the trucking crowd.

If you are anywhere near a big city, finding a single parking spot after early in the afternoon can be rough, especially if you are a new driver. Some of the parking spots you will come on are virtually impossible for a rookie to attempt and chances are you really don't want to.

If you drive at night, chances are better at finding a good parking spot in the morning left by an early riser. And, since you are a day early and just 3 miles from your delivery point, you will pull right in to a good parking spot, have all day to catch up on your sleep, visit the showering facility, and then consume a massive quantity of that very delicious "all you can eat" buffet food. More later on aggressive avoidance of the "all you can eat" buffet.

When you begin a trip, careful planning is necessitated. There is nothing complicated about this. It just becomes part of your routine and the more you do it the easier it gets. If you are going somewhere you have been several times before, you will start to feel comfortable about it. You know how long it takes to get there, when and where you will stop for fuel, where you like to eat, where you can park, and most importantly where you will have access to the facilities.

Yes, the facilities indeed. There are few worse things on the road than when you have to "go" and you are sitting in the middle of rush hour on I-70 in St. Louis. I will always remember listening to a guy on the CB, who said he had stopped at a local convenience store and bought a very delicious burrito, and was now begging anyone listening to tell him where he could get off the highway so he could "go." It was really funny to listen to at the time, but wait until it happens to you. And, it will. Bet on it. Plan ahead or suffer the consequences.

As you drive about the country you need to make mental notes of many things, even in places you are not stopping. Remember that little truck stop outside of Earle, Arkansas, that had lots of parking at 2 in the morning, even though you are headed to Memphis. You may be back there in a few days or weeks. You never know when. But, knowing that you are getting very tired and you are just ten miles from a place you know you can park for the night can be very comforting. Trust me on that.

There are certain states that don't mind if you park on the on or off ramps to the interstate. You will notice the trucks already parking there and you will notice that very often there is plenty of room to get your rig completely off the road and go to sleep.

There are also some places where it is not allowed. If you are on the road for awhile you will just start knowing where you can stop. Always keep your eyes open. Pay attention now and it will pay off later on down the road. You can usually get away with what you see the other drivers doing, but not always. That is why you must watch what is going on around you at all times, if you want to stay in your comfort zone and away from all the "professional citation writers." Yes, I am referring to the local constabulary. You do not want to park where you will be ticketed by the DOT officers, local police, or even the local meter maid. It will most likely be expensive.

Sometimes you have to learn the hard way. I remember driving through Virginia in the middle of the night after coming all the way from New England. I was getting a bit drowsy, but the few times I passed a truck stop, I noticed one thing, no parking spaces anywhere. Not one.

I finally came to a rest area and pulled in. To my delight there were all kinds of parking spaces. I thought this was great, until I pulled into a space, stopped, and read the happy little sign posted directly in front of me. It said, "MAXIMUM 2 HOURS PARKING." Unbelievable!

Being that I needed about ten hours of sleep, that would not work. That being said, I might have taken a chance and hoped nobody was out writing tickets in the middle of the night. However, I like to sleep comfortably, so I drove a while longer to my destination and found a parking space right on the street in front of my delivery point.

Fortunately, many places to which you deliver do have plenty of parking, either on their property or on the street next to their facility, but not always. I was lucky, because I was getting very tired at that point. That is why careful planning is essential to the safe and successful conclusion of your journeys.

That is also why some drivers like to hook up with "dedicated routes." This is where you are pretty much going to the same places every time. They usually pay a little less, but when you take into account the aggravation factor of constantly driving to unfamiliar places, and dealing with a multitude of surprises like nowhere to park, it can be worth it. There are solutions to most of the problems in the trucking biz. There are many options and this can be one of them.

I actually took one of those very driving positions with a company, one of those very visible companies that you see frequently around the country. I spotted a driver wanted ad in the San Diego Union Tribune newspaper. It said "Wanted,

Class A CDL Driver for I-5 Dedicated." This paid a little less than I was accustomed to, so I really had to think about this one for a minute.

The deciding factors here were that they told me that I would be taking two loads each day from Los Angeles to San Diego and back on Interstate 5. That was acceptable. Additionally, they had a ridiculously secure parking facility in Fontana with a ten foot high stone wall surrounding it and you even needed a specially coded security card with your picture on it just to get in. This appeared to be an impenetrable fortress that was secure from all but a nuclear holocaust or perhaps a 9.2 earth quake. So I decided to give it a shot.

What could I possibly have to lose? Hmmm.

So I parked my car at their terminal in Fontana, took a cab to the airport, and had a short plane ride to their terminal in Phoenix, where they held their orientation. I then went through the same process which I described to you previously. They actually had me listed right on their identity sheet as "driver for I-5 dedicated." They actually knew what I was there for. Right?

After spending several days going through their orientation, I was assigned to a truck. Now these trucks, which appeared to be well maintained, brightly colored, and clean vehicles, were actually quite deceptive. Upon closer inspection, these fancy trucks were missing parts and other things of note.

I was told that my truck had just undergone a rigorous two week inspection and maintenance check up and it was fully road worthy. It did run, but aside from that, they lied. My first clue to the inadequacies of this company came in the form of a new mattress. What? Believe it or not, there is some sort of stipulation in DOT regulations that require a company to provide new drivers with a new mattress. I wasn't really aware of this and really didn't care anyway. The only problem with this was that they expected the drivers to take the old mattresses out of their truck and drag them all the way across the terminal to where they would be disposed of and then come and get their own new mattress.

Truck mattresses aren't especially heavy, but when you are required to carry them clear across the terminal and then attempt to make them fit through the door of your truck and get them into the rear of the cab, it becomes an irritation worthy of note. This is especially true in a place like Phoenix, where the day time temperature is rarely in the cool range.

Not all drivers are physically adept enough to be attempting this, let alone the fact that this is something the company maintenance department should have been doing. Screw this cheap ass lazy company for welcoming their new drivers by allowing them to haul some nasty dirty old mattresses around that were left by the previous drivers, who probably also quit out of disgust. This was something they damn well should have done themselves before I or any of the other potential laborers ever got there. They just didn't want to pay anyone to do it.

Drivers are generally just getting paid just for miles driven and not for free laboring service. If your company starts expecting you to provide free services with regularity, they should in fact become suspect. Take note.

This should have been a red flag to me, but I've had to do worse things than haul around an old bug infested mattress. After scrounging around and coming up with a few extra parts, that I needed for the safe operation of my truck, I grabbed a trailer and headed off to my first shipper. Oh and by the way, as I was instructed, these parts were taken off other trucks in their yard. I am certain these trucks were to be assigned, without the needed repairs, to other drivers. With what I had seen already, there was little doubt that this would be the case.

I picked up a relatively heavy load of something or other and was now on my way to California, to begin my happy affiliation with an Interstate 5 dedicated route. Yes indeed, some easy stuff.

When you are in Phoenix, the roads are all relatively flat, but as you head west into California on Interstate 8, you run into some mountainous terrain. In other words you are going up the hill. As I started up the hill I noticed that most assuredly the RPM's on my tachometer were advancing, where as my speedometer was not performing in unison as expected. In fact you could feel the transmission slipping out of gear and the engine just revving up higher.

In summation, I became well aware that the two week inspection, maintenance, and check up for my truck was just as it now appeared, a lie! Any real mechanic who had thoroughly gone over this truck would have known that the clutch, among other ignored problems, was completely useless.

Clearly they had done virtually nothing to make sure this was a safe, well maintained, and roadworthy vehicle. I battled with this nice truck over the next several days, so that I could successfully deliver my load and then get to the Freightliner Dealer in Fontana. I got there, dropped off the truck, and went to visit the local motel for a few days and of course this was at the company's expense.

It took eleven days for the Freightliner dealer to replace the clutch and several other items that were necessary to make this truck legal to operate as a commercial vehicle. The itemized list of things that were required to make this truck right was three pages long and the bill was for over $3,000. For a company to have told me their lies about the two weeks of maintenance, it should have really been an eye opening clue as to their incompetence. However, I was really still looking forward to my dedicated position on Interstate 5. Thus on we went.

For the next several weeks after the return of my truck I took repeated loads up and down Interstate 5. The problem with this was that I had to remind them every single lousy time, that I was hired for a dedicated position on Interstate 5. They were incapable of remembering this minor detail even once.

They tried to send me to Las Vegas, Salt Lake City, Phoenix, and several other places. None of these have anything whatsoever to do with Interstate 5. I don't mind going to any of these illustrious vacation spots, but I could do this for any company out there and get paid more to do it. Never once did I get a load from Los Angeles to San Diego as I was told I would be doing twice each day.

I finally grew weary of their incompetence. I only took this position because of I-5 and certainly they had been reminded constantly of it. Not only did this fun filled escapade pay less than I would have normally accepted, they operated on a graduated scale. Shorter loads would pay a couple cents more. Conveniently every stinking load they gave me would be just 3 or 4 miles over into the next pay zone. Thus, I was always paid two cents per mile less by a very small margin. It was without exception always in their favor.

I actually stayed with them for a total of about five weeks before informing them that I had had enough of their marvelous company and their constant lies. All they ever said was that they had to send their drivers where the loads were located. That would have been fine if it had paid more and if they had not hired me for one reason, a dedicated position on Interstate 5. This is not complicated and yet they were incapable of figuring it out.

This was a company that was obviously convinced they could sucker drivers into whatever they wanted them to do. In many cases I'm sure they get exactly that. Not from me. See ya!

Just for the record, this was the same nice company that claimed that I abandoned their truck. It was in fact left exactly where I had previously agreed in writing to leave it, at their terminal in Fontana, and where my car was securely parked behind the ten foot high impenetrable fortress.

I am certain that the way they treat their drivers, they probably feel the necessity for such a facility out of fear of driver retaliation. I however had no interest in pay back for their sorry excuse of a truck, their lousy company, or the pathetic treatment I received over five weeks of lies. My truck number was 2020 and clearly the vision from my truck was infinitely clearer than the vision of this company as to how to run a successful business with contented drivers. So much for this explanation. On now to more productive matters.

On The Road Again

3. Log Books & Weigh Stations

There are certain things that come with the job of a "professional tourist" that you would rather not deal with, and yet they have become prevalent if not necessary. We are going to deal with a few of them. They can be an irritation and incessantly annoying and yet they are a part of reality in the world of truck driving.

Why do drivers have log books? Answer, to piss you off of course. They are in existence so that the Department of Transportation officers can find out what you have been up to. They are also there for the DOT officers to find out if you even know what you have been up to. They also make an additional source of revenue for the state in which you got a ticket for not filling out your log book the way the DOT officer says is the correct way to do it. In English, that means that if a DOT officer wants to write you a ticket, chances are excellent that he will find that you have made mistakes in your log book preparation. In reality, that is probably easy to do if they want to.

There are numerous ways to fill out your log book, but only one true right way. That way is the one in which the DOT officer, that is currently inspecting your log book, says it is. Never argue with the DOT officers! You can plead insanity, beg for mercy, ask for a stay of execution, but whatever you do, do not argue with the DOT dudes! Period!

As a "professional tourist" you will probably have frequent contact with DOT officers and usually this will be at the weigh station you are about to pass through. You have most likely just successfully navigated your rig through the scale and are preparing to be happily on your way, when the sign that previously said to "Proceed at 5 mph," has magically changed to "Park and bring in your paperwork." Instant terror fills your veins as your blood pressure soars to previously unattained levels and your mind fills with visions of out of service orders and huge overweight ticket fines. It is absolutely the fear of the unknown which now encompasses your existence. Prepare for death. It is at hand.

So you pull your rig over and grab your shipping papers, permit book, CDL, medical card, trailer registration (it's probably hiding in the little box at the front of your trailer), and the infamous log book and head on in to the weigh station office. What you will do next is take several slow deep breaths and relax. In through the nose and out through the mouth. In through the nose and out through the mouth. It is very relaxing.

When you enter the office, you will be friendly and cheerful, and you will greet the DOT officer who has requested your presence. You will look him in the eye. Do not look as though you have just driven 900 non stop miles (even though you just did), and give them exactly what they ask for. I repeat. Give them exactly what they ask for, and no more. Treat this as an IRS audit. As the experts in IRS audits will tell you, do not volunteer any excess information. Just shut the hell up and do only as requested, and your potential for a successful DOT evaluation will increase dramatically.

The chances are excellent that all they want is to check your current registration, IFTA card, and maybe your proof of insurance. You really never know until you get in the door what will be required. Actually there is no harm in initiating a friendly discussion. Just do not volunteer any extras (In other words, if you are in

Colorado, do not tell the DOT inspector about your very delicious dinner last night in Atlanta).

You will be asking for trouble when he tries to figure out how you drove over 1300 miles in such a short time. Then you can explain how you just drove 24 straight hours without rest. That should go over well. Thus, I say that if you are not supremely confident in your conversational abilities, just shut the hell up and follow directions. And by all means be professional and courteous.

There are several levels of DOT inspections that as a driver you will inevitably come face to face with. Either way, the chances are excellent that the DOT guy has every right to do exactly what he tells you he is going to do. The fact is that most (not all) of these folks are very friendly and are actually just doing their job. I would not want that job. It has got to be rough knowing that you are the last thing that any driver wants to deal with on the road. "Oh no, the dreaded DOT dudes."

Most likely if they want to inspect you and they did not come running out of the office and come right up to your truck, you are at most only going to be visited with a Level 3 inspection. This means they want to check your papers (This is not the Gestapo. Don't worry). They want to check your CDL, your medical card, the other previously mentioned items, and of course the infamous log book.

However, because you are a well prepared "professional tourist," you are going to sail through the inspection and leave with a nice little paper, that says you have "passed the audition" and done so without any violations. Turn this paper over to your company and sometimes they will pay you a small amount of money. You should probably check in advance on that, but it does make the company look good, when you successfully pass the test, so they are sometimes willing to reward a good report by throwing you a small bone. Don't quote me on this though. They may not.

If on the other hand, as you pull up to the scale, the sneaky DOT guy comes up to your truck, jumps up on the side, sticking his snoopy head in the window, prepare for a more thorough check up. This may be your official Level 1 inspection.

"Oh no, what the hell do you do now? You are doomed!" Probably the first thing he or she (watch out for that mean DOT woman at the north bound Temecula, CA weigh station and border check point) will ask for is your log book. They want it immediately so you do not have a chance to fix anything.

NEVER go into a weigh station without having a currently prepared log book. You are asking for trouble. Even if it can be equated to the official "Book of Lies," do not enter that facility until your book is current to your last change of duty. The two most important things in regard to preparation are neatness (if they can't read it, it may require further investigation), and being current.

I am not going into how to fill out your damn log book. They will spend extensive time on such matters at truck school and at your company orientation. I will only say that before you even think about going near any weighing facility, be sure that miserable little book is neat and up to date. That is essential to your avoidance of a disastrous DOT inspection.

A few companies will provide you with paperless logs. In other words it is electronically tied to your Qualcom (satellite communication unit). This means your opportunities to cheat are dramatically diminished. I have heard that some of these paperless monsters will actually shut down your engine if you go over your allotted driving hours. Ahh the wonders of technology, and as the years go by I am certain it will get worse. I do not recommend such companies for obvious reasons.

Some drivers have been known to have a second and fallacious "back up" log book. Only a complete idiot would bother with this. It takes long enough just to fill out one book. Any fool who would actually take the time to fill out two of these deserves to get caught and beaten mercilessly with a rubber hose.

The Level 1 inspection is the most thorough of all. The inspector is going to get under your truck, measuring different things and checking to make sure all the working parts are in good working order. He will also hang a rope from the top of your trailer and swing back and forth making chimpanzee noises. Uhhh, alright maybe not quite that extensive.

You may be questioned orally in regard to the operation of various aspects of your vehicle and maybe even about where you have just driven from. Don't get tripped up because nothing here is complicated. You are going to be asked to do complicated things like flash your flashers and blow your horn. This stuff better be working because as a competent professional, you always do a daily inspection of all these items. Right?

In reality, I rarely see drivers do their daily inspections as required by the DOT. In fact judging by the rare physical specimens that often pass as drivers, I am truly amazed that some of them can even climb down from the cab of their rigs. I know damn well these folks are less likely to check everything as required.

Every time I get fuel, use the rest room, get out to eat, or any time I am waiting to get loaded or unloaded I will walk around the whole rig and check for obvious faults. It is just a habit and if you do it five times in a day, you needed the exercise anyway. You cannot perform this act too many times. You never know when something will turn up and require immediate attention. This is not like your everyday four wheeler. You need to know if things are less than perfect. You are responsible legally for everything. If you get in a wreck, because a large piece of metal has been dangling from the under side of your trailer and you failed to notice, it is your fault.

As a driver you are probably not a mechanic. I know I am not and have no intention whatsoever of becoming one. A competent mechanic is a rare commodity and is fully deserving of a driver's respect and admiration. If I have to perform mechanics, it is in regard to changing a light bulb or dumping a gallon of Rotella into the crankcase. But, sooner or later you will have a tire blow out because of low air pressure. This is something that you can readily observe in advance. Low tire pressure and the 46,000 lbs of Budweiser you are hauling will cause frequent annihilation of a recapped tire.

The fact that the majority of trailer tires are recapped means that they are going to have an increasing chance of falling apart. Look at all the tire treads (gators = essential CB terminology) you pass on the highway. They can be dangerous especially when a happy little 4 wheeler is tailgating you and one of those babies explodes into a large uncontrollable projectile.

Yes indeed, I was cruising up Highway 287 in Colorado, with one of those shiny new yellow VW Bugs riding right on my bumper. This guy would not pass and just wanted to stay right on me (maybe he was saving fuel like a drafting NASCAR driver). Whatever he was doing, he was clearly terrified when that big ole gator came shooting out from the back of my trailer. From that point on I don't think he came within a quarter mile of my DOT bumper.

But getting back to your Level 1 inspection, checking little things like flashers and tire pressure can save you from getting jammed by an unhappy DOT inspector. If it ever gets to the point where I have to perform serious mechanics, I will put a wrap on driving altogether.

One other important note. When you do your daily inspection, which you will note in the daily log, make sure you do not put it down until late in the day. In the event you are inspected by the DOT and you are showing that you just did your vehicle inspection in the last hour, you may have trouble explaining why your headlight is out and the left rear turn signal is no longer functional. Much easier to say you haven't done your daily inspection yet and it certainly wasn't like that yesterday. Was it?

Assuming that you work for a company that actually takes some pride in proper maintenance procedures and makes sure your truck is in good legal operating order, and also assuming that you have done your part in making sure all your papers are current, you are going to pass your Level 1. When you do, the DOT dude will put a happenin' little sticker on your window and tell you to have a nice day. You will then say "Thank you" and be on your way. Get in the truck and drive out of the weigh station. Do not stop to make a quick phone call, a peanut butter and jelly sandwich, or anything else. You have survived the inspection. Do not give them the opportunity to come back for more. Thank your lucky stars and "get the hell out of Dodge."

Nothing against Dodge City, but I have to say that once you have driven through Dodge City, Kansas and taken a deep breath of that fresh air coming from the local meat packing facilities, you will no longer wonder where that saying came from. Depending on how long you are there, it will be something you will carry in your lungs for days and a memory that will last a lifetime. Bet on that.

Elaborating further on the virtues of the illustrious weigh station. Aggressive avoidance is of the essence here. The more weigh stations you enter, the more you increase your potential for disaster. I am not saying that you should look for ways to go around the weigh station. I have only done that once and it was an accident. I missed the turn. Errr, uhhh, no I really did. Seriously.

What I am saying is that if you happen to know that certain weighing facilities are closed at 9pm every night, why not take advantage of that instead of tempting fate. As you drive past a closed weigh station, you will frequently observe trucks that have parked for the night just past the scale. Once you are through, you are home free. At least you might be inclined to think so. I prefer to drive on a bit further.

Another one of those essential questions to ask your potential recruiter is, "Do you use Prepass?" Prepass is a little black box that you stick on your windshield and as you approach numerous weigh stations, it gives you authorization to bypass. Let me say that without question, when that little light beeps green it is very soothing.

When it beeps out a red signal, you have to pull in and are definitely wondering why they are pulling you in, especially when all you are hauling is 10k lbs of insulation. Either way, I have saved incredible amounts of time by being able to frequently bypass the weigh stations. Prepass is an asset, unless of course you have a cheapass company that will give it to you, but then expects you to pay them back for using it. Yes, I worked for one of those companies also (sorry no names again). I think it might be a dollar or so for each time it is used. Either way I am not paying for it.

Generally weigh stations are just that. They are a necessary and time consuming evil that must check to be sure you are not carrying too much weight for the highways. As long as the scale shows you are less than 12k lbs on the steers (front tires), less than 34k lbs on each of your trailer axles, and less than 80k lbs total weight, you should have no problem. This is for the standard 53 foot trailer. Other size trailers have different limits, but this is what you are most likely to be operating with as a new driver.

This brings into play another fun item with which a driver may have to do regular battle. It is the ceremonial sliding of the tandems. It is an official rite of passage and an event to be immortalized. NOT!! If anything in trucking sucks as bad as having to slide the tandems to adjust to the correct and legal axle weight, this is right up there in the top two (the other being the time honored application of the chains to the drive wheels in a raging blizzard when it is 10 degrees below zero outside your cab)! Sometimes it is a very smooth process. Other times it is an impossibility.

Without going into the specifics of the process, I will say that it is often easier to do this with an empty trailer. You must in fact be a masterful guesser and the person loading your trailer must be something more than a complete imbecile. With a little practice you can become a reliable guesser. Those who load the trailers are most often completely out of your control.

The tandems must not only be set for the legal weight limits, but when you are in a place such as California, you best not set them too far or the California DOT folks will write you a cute little summons that will cost you a small fortune for an over length trailer. I feel certain this is something you will never forget. Thankfully I have managed to avoid getting any of these.

Your company should clue you in to the exact regulations and settings for the trailers they are using. However, if they do not, it is you the driver that will be responsible for your ticket. In fact any damn thing that does go wrong is the responsibility of the professional in charge of the operation of that vehicle.

That is why you should familiarize yourself with the Cat or other such scale facilities usually located at your nearest truck stop. Your company will most likely reimburse you for your expense, but you will have to deal with the aggravation of sliding the tandems. It is something you will have to do frequently, so get used to it early.

Only once have I suffered a complete inability to slide the tandems, and it did in fact take four professional mechanics at the Ontario, California TA truck stop to jack up the back of my fully loaded trailer and slide those bastards into submission. They did it in just under 2 hours. Have I emphasized the fact that sliding the tandems truly sucks? Repetition again.

A final note on weigh stations. If you drive at night, not only are the weigh stations more likely to be closed, they are also much less likely to be doing those happy little Level 1 inspections in the dark.

That being said. Again, almost nothing is 100% guaranteed. I drove right up to a weigh station in Utah late at night, only to be pulled in for a Level 3 check of the paperwork. I was very tired and it didn't matter to me one way or another at that point. The DOT officer was very friendly and we had a little chat about all the autographs that decorated their station walls and I was on my way in about ten minutes.

Another thing that is a certainty is that you never know

when you will come upon the infamous "mystery weight station." It is an ominous experience and one which can take place any damn place the DOT dudes want it. They can set up their portable scales pretty much anywhere they want as long as they have a little room at the side of the road. On more than a few occasions I have been driving out in the middle of nowhere when I have come upon that friendly little sign that says, "Weigh Station Ahead, All Commercial Vehicles Must Exit."

Not too long ago as I was traveling south on Interstate 25 going from Colorado into New Mexico, and passing through the weigh station I spotted something out of the corner of my eye. This is where I will again repeat to you the importance of paying attention to things you see for future benefit.

I just happened to see a big truck on the northbound side of the highway and for all intents and purposes, it appeared to be the subject of a SWAT team offensive. There were in fact four DOT officers swarming over this truck like ants on a candy bar. I took note of this because I saw the DOT van sitting in the corner and I knew, because of previous experience that they like to be real sneaky in New Mexico.

Keeping this in mind, a week or so later when I returned on the northbound side of I-25, I stopped at a rest area just a few miles south of my previous DOT sighting. I proceeded to make my log book very neat and current. I then drove on a few more miles and to my surprise there was that friendly sign for the "mystery weigh station."

I pulled in and right away the friendly New Mexico DOT officer walked up to my truck and said, "Do you have a log book?" I replied in the affirmative and handed it to him. He looked at it for several seconds, handed it back to me and said, "Have a nice day." I thanked him and was on my way.

The point here is that, had I not been aware that there was a huge possibility that I was about to run into the "mystery weigh station," I might not have had a current log book, and who knows what other perils that would have opened me up to. When he asked for the log book, he wasn't worried about whether my truck was in good shape or not. He was there for one reason. He wanted to create revenue for the state of New Mexico by writing tickets. The easiest ticket to write is for a log book violation. At any given moment I would bet a very high percentage of truck drivers are not quite current with their log books. In fact many of them are several days or more behind at a time. Bet on it.

Take this seriously, when I tell you to always pay attention to what is going on around you, even though it doesn't affect you today. Be sure and make a mental note, because you never know what's going on, when you come back the other way. Hey that rhymes. Maybe I'll become a poet, or not.

Truck parked at a closed weigh station in Oregon. Closed is always the best way to observe a weighing facility, especially in Oregon, where there is no such thing as quarter or a sympathetic DOT officer. Take note.

The Author returning the remains of a recapped trailer tire to the company. Yes, they do want them back.

On The Road Again

4. CB's, Cell Phones, Qualcoms, Communications

When you are out there in the middle of nowhere, the more potential communication you have the better, or so it might seem. I'm probably not the best source for a discussion on the virtues of modern communications as my preference is to use them as little as possible. When I first started driving I didn't get a CB (Citizen's Band 2 way Radio) until I had built up enough points on my TA Frequent Fueler Card. It took nearly seven months. And guess what? I didn't miss it a bit. No, in reality you can get along without one, but they do come in handy.

You will occasionally need them to call one of your shippers or receivers to let them know you are there and for them to open the gate and let you in, or some other such important thing. They are also good to find out if the chicken coupes (high level trucker CB terminology for the weigh stations) are open. Hearing that the local coupe is shut down and nobody at home can cause mild relief.

It is also occasionally worthwhile to know that the "Smokey's" or the "county Mounties" or the "Evel Knievel's" are on the prowl and taking pictures. In other words, various police organizations are clocking your speed with the radar unit. In places like Oregon and Ohio where the speed limit is 55 for trucks and they like to write tickets to truck drivers, it can be very useful. Like Sammy Hagar said in the song "I Can't Drive 55."

A CB can also be useful when you are broken down on the side of the road. And, do not be naïve; the chances of a breakdown are very high. I don't care how new your truck is. Sooner or later there is a high probability that you too will find yourself sitting on the side of the road waiting for a mechanic or a tow truck or both. It is just part of the reality of truck life and the more forms of communication to which you have access, the better off you will be.

The plain truth is that most of the frivolous banter that passes through your CB is completely useless. It is senseless drivel espoused by bored or ignorant drivers, who are generally letting you know that they have very little to offer in regard to intelligent conversation. It is one thing to carry on a legitimate communication between drivers, but too often it digresses into an "I'll kick your ass," type situation by people who never have any intention of meeting. The moronic talk goes back and forth until you come to the realization that you are wasting your time listening to nonsense.

I always find it humorous how many tough guy drivers there are out on the road, but when you get into a truck stop, drivers say almost nothing to each other. Personally, other than talking to shippers and receivers on occasion, I have probably actually spoken over the CB less times than you can count on one hand.

The best reason to have the CB on is to inform you as to traffic conditions in front of you. It could be a lifesaver on a foggy road or in a blizzard. You could be sitting in a ten mile back up and need to know which lane to be in. Then again, most people on the road don't have a CB. So if you are on the road and don't have it "on," it is not the end of the world. Most of the time I carry a small handheld CB that plugs into the cigarette lighter. If I need it, it is good for a short distance and only picks up what is being said in the nearby vicinity. As far as I'm concerned, that is all I need or want.

That being said I will relate a short story I heard a few years back in Wisconsin while sitting at a receiver and waiting to get unloaded. About a month before there had been a major accident along a major highway, which included an exploding tanker truck. It was on the national news.

The driver relating the incident had been lucky enough to get his truck stopped. It was a very foggy night and as the fog goes, you are often completely unable to see what is at the end of your truck hood let alone what is going on twenty feet ahead on the roadway. Numerous cars and trucks ran into each other, one after another, including this tanker which exploded. Lives were lost.

The driver told the story of how he and a police officer were completely unable to get to a car in which a young girl was trapped. The horrendous heat and flames made it impossible. The truck driver graphically mentioned watching this poor victim's blond hair being engulfed in flames and he was completely helpless to assist. He said that he had screamed at the officer to shoot her and put her out of her misery. Naturally, that wasn't a possibility and she suffered a painful end. That story sticks with me as I am certain it will always be with the driver who witnessed it.

You certainly do wonder if it would have made a difference had all those drivers had a CB on and received an advance warning of what was ahead. There are most definitely times when having a radio proves useful.

Moving on to the ever present cell phone, I will say little. Is there anyone that does not have one? The problem is that too many people think they can drive and talk at the same time. Many of these people can't chew gum and drive at the same time. To those "multi tasking" pea wits, I say, "get off the road before making calls, you imbecile."

Too many times have I witnessed a driver doing something absurd, only to pull along side and view this moron in mid conversation on the cell phone. Chances are really big, that you can not really be attentive to the realities of the road, when you are concentrating on the person at the other end of your call. Every day people are in wrecks because they were chatting away as they rammed right into another vehicle. Do it in a big rig and you could end up being charged with murder.

In a few states it is illegal to be on your cell phone when driving. I am rarely on my cell phone at all, and yet I confess to having been on the cell in New York City of all places. New York City? Yes! Another driver was calling to tell me how to get to the Arthur Ashe Tennis Stadium from where I was in the toll line at the George Washington Bridge. It was very uncomfortable trying to write directions, talk on the phone, and keep from running over the top of a thousand crazed minivan and SUV drivers at the same time. However, it was necessary.

I suspect that most such calls rank right up there with the usefulness of the average CB conversation, but some times it must be done. Do it just because you have to use up your monthly 10,000 any time minutes with mindless babbling and it could prove costly.

Finally we get to that marvel of technology, your satellite communication device. Frequently known as a Qualcom and as I stated earlier it appears mostly to be so your company can keep track of you. It sometimes will not function when you have a roof over the top of your truck, such as at the fuel island of the truck stop. Or, if you want to be sneaky, you can wrap aluminum foil around the little satellite dish attached to the top of your truck. I don't know if that really works because I have never tried it. Just a rumor.

When a company supplies you with a QC (Qualcom) unit, this allows the transmittal of both important and sometimes useless and irritating information. It can be used to transmit your load information back and forth. It allows you to inform the company that you are ready for your next load, or even request important things such as with the infamous "time off" macro (satellite message).

It also lets the company know, within a short distance, your current location. They do like to know if you are going a few miles out of your "designated route" to visit your girl friend, your mother, or even the local Wal Mart to stock up on junk food. They know what you are doing. Sometimes I think they have a video camera in the back of your cab, so they can film your every move. I'm sure they've often pondered such intrusions on your privacy.

It can also be used to let your company know that your truck is broken down and stopped in the middle of Interstate 880 going into Oakland in the middle of the afternoon rush hour. Judging from personal experience, your emergency macro sent to the company is of little more than a consolation to you as a driver, knowing that you have in fact informed the company of your dire and life threatening circumstances. I have very definitely gotten the feeling, that when you send one of these messages, ain't nobody paying even the smallest bit of attention. You are on your own, bud.

Too often it will take repeated messages on the QC, several cell calls to the company, a few pleas of terror over the CB to any drivers, who might be listening, and the official embarrassment of the 10 mile traffic back up caused by you, because you did not manage to get the damn truck off the road before it shut down. This stuff happens every day to drivers around the country and it can happen to you too.

Yes indeed, the QC has numerous uses. It also has a happy little obnoxious beep, that is often impossible to get rid of, when the company wants to let you know about some truly essential and timely information in regard to a new fuel stop in New Jersey being added to your list of designated stops. This announcement will most likely come at 7AM eastern time, just when you have fallen asleep after driving half way across the country. In this case it is an irritant. You will of course be in California on Pacific Time. So this nice little tone will be sure and wake you up at 4 in the morning. And because you think it may be important, you will get up and check it. If you don't, it will keep beeping intermittently until the end of time. The reality of these communication devices is that sometimes they are invariably useless.

It is always the responsibility of the driver to deal with whatever comes up on the road. If you break down out in the middle of nowhere, what will you do? Not all companies supply you with the QC unit. They have to pay for it and cheap bastards are often what they are at the driver's expense. Do you think you will have cell phone service everywhere you go? And how 'bout that CB? Do you imagine that there is always someone out there listening? The answers are a resounding "NO" and "HELL NO!"

Not long ago, I was making a delivery to Pagosa Springs, Colorado in an almost new Volvo. I drove across Wolf Creek Pass. This is up in the mountains and very definitely out in the sticks of southwestern Colorado. Although this is a very scenic area for vacationing and such (a "professional tourist's" delight), it is also very rural. There was construction going on at the top of the pass and I was told when I first drove through, that if I didn't make my return trip before 7 PM, they shut down the highway and I would be stuck waiting there until the next morning. As quickly as possible, I managed to get to my destination, get unloaded, and then head back from whence I had come. I blazed on my return trip so as to be able to get past the construction before the deadline. As I came to within a couple miles of the construction, my nearly new Volvo warned me (the ever present idiot lights), that it was going to shut down.

With only minutes to spare before the deadline, I was not anticipating this at all. I was thinking only of getting across Wolf Creek Pass. I had been going up a steep incline for quite a few miles and in reality there was absolutely no place to get off the road on this two lane highway. What do you do? You panic! Alright, not really. You hope you can make it to the next pullout. I did not.

My happy little unit decided to over heat and shut down right in the middle of the highway. Such things do happen. I put the emergency flashers on and attempted several things. The truck would not restart right away, so I decided to call for assistance. With a company that doesn't supply a QC unit you must try an alternative method. Guess what? With two cell phones, you might hope that one would work. NOT! No 911 or any service whatsoever in the area. Let's see. Try the old standby. Maybe someone is listening on the CB. No! I am convinced that no one in the vicinity of Pagosa Springs, Colorado listens to the CB.

Knowing that in a few minutes this highway would be shut down for the night and that there would be no more traffic and no chance to get any assistance at least until the next morning, something had to be done now. I did manage to get it started and get another half mile to a nice pullout area before it over heated and shut down again. However, I was on my own and with no way to communicate with any one who could assist me.

As it was getting dark it was time to act or suffer the

consequences. Getting out my flash light, I opened the hood and immediately noticed the mangled broken fan belt. This was the cause of the over heating. I also decided that since I had just come about fifteen miles up the hill from Pagosa Springs, and going further up the hill was not an option, that I was going to make a gallant attempt to go back down the hill. Amazing! Going down the hill the truck didn't over heat at all.

Here again, the moral of the story, aside from a bit of luck, is that acting quickly and logically I managed to get back down the hill to Pagosa Springs and to the repair shop without counting on the assistance of any one but myself. That was the only real choice. Sometimes you have to make tough choices quickly. You are going to be in charge too. What will you do under similar circumstances?

I then spent the next several days (at company expense) vacationing in Pagosa Springs, sampling local cuisine and such, and having a thoroughly memorable time while waiting for a new fan belt to arrive. Although this was not in my original play book, I managed to get some needed time off. This is called turning a negative into a positive and created a truly rewarding experience. Some times that is what you have to do. YEAH!!

Had I not acted quickly and logically, I could have spent a substantial amount of time at the top of Wolf Creek Pass feeling sorry for myself. Had this been in the middle of a raging snow storm I could have been screwed. This of course brings up potential survival techniques. You have to be prepared for all eventualities.

Always keep as much fuel as possible in your tanks. If you get stuck in ten feet of snow and it's twenty below zero, with no assistance for a week, you can run that engine and keep warm. Also, the more times you stop for fuel, the more showers you will accumulate on your frequent fueler cards. The more free showers you accumulate the better. There are few things nastier than standing in a long line in back of some foul smelling truck driver, who clearly has not visited the showers any time in the recent past. Frequent use of truck stop showering facilities is a very necessary survival technique. Make no mistake about that.

Always be sure and have a supply of junk food and plenty of fresh water. You never know what can happen out there and if you aren't prepared, you can bet your ass it will happen. Something as simple as no parking at the local truck stop can cause you to miss a meal. However, you will be prepared with an ample supply of very delicious junk food, apples, bananas, and whatever excites you. Skipping a regular meal should not be the end of the world for most drivers and probably is most beneficial for some.

Planning ahead can save your life or more than likely just make you comfortable. Do not count on anybody but yourself. Forget the CB, the cell phone, or the QC. All your communication devices are conveniences. Don't rely on them for necessities. What will always matter is that you have prepared yourself for those bad things that will eventually pay you a visit on the road. Pay attention and hang on to your life.

On The Road Again

5. Directions, Or Do They Seriously Expect You To Get There?

One of the most important aspects of driving is also probably the most neglected aspect of driving. Rest assured that your company has taken the utmost care to be sure the directions you receive to your shippers and receivers have been accurately and precisely coordinated such that there is a very small probability that you will have any difficulty whatsoever arriving at your appointed destination in a timely manner. NOT!! Not even a remote chance of that most of the time.

With the availability of such incredible technology on the Internet alone in regard to driving directions to and from various destinations, it is absolutely incredible the lack of care that is taken in regard to supplying drivers with accurate directions. It is downright pathetic.

Many companies continue to send their drivers out with the same incorrect directions that they have used for who knows how many years. It doesn't matter whether or not they have been informed by drivers that the directions are just wrong. It just seems that nobody other than a driver has any concern about it. It never gets changed and driver after driver gets the same wrong directions and sooner or later many of them come to the same conclusion. If none of these dispatchers or other supposedly responsible employees give a damn, I won't either. And of course they eventually move on to another company, where they can be equally dissatisfied by a lack of attention to detail or even a remote semblance of driver consideration or respect.

Not all companies are guilty of this and some in fact provide very detailed directions, but this is the exception. It is an embarrassment, with the available technology, that any companies provide their drivers with anything but detailed and accurate directions. The most important thing in trucking, aside from driver safety, is the most incredibly overlooked.

I wonder how many thousands of times deliveries been late, how many trucks have been damaged because they were sent down a road where they could not safely turn around, and how many accidents have been caused simply on behalf of lame half-assed directions.

How intelligent is it for a company to supply a driver with directions telling him to turn left where they are supposed to turn right? How hard is it to look up on the Internet and see that it is 2.3 miles to Oak Street, rather than just say turn at Oak Street, not having even a remote idea where Oak Street might be.

Wrong directions should be a thing of the past and yet in my recent experience companies continue to provide their most valuable commodity (their drivers) with inaccurate and even unsafe directions. I was once directed down a highway in upstate New York and told turn left at another highway. It took awhile before I found it on the map. My company supplied directions would have you believe that the turn was right up the road and yet it was 211 miles to that turn off. This is another one of those well known companies, which shall remain nameless. It is most certainly a company with enough of a reputation that you would think they would have enough professionalism to supply their drivers with accurate directions. They didn't and I'm sure they still couldn't care less.

Most often drivers are going to destinations they have

never been before. Just one wrong turn can put a tractor trailer down a dead end street with no place to turn around. What happens then? How many drivers get so discouraged from receiving endless inaccurate directions that they quit. Driver turnover is already ridiculously high at well over 100% annually for some companies and yet they make little effort to fix problems.

Another time and only a few short months after I started driving, I was headed to a receiver in Iowa. I followed my directions exactly as given. I got off the main highway as directed and proceeded to take the first right turn. It was about 4AM and even though it was still dark out I hadn't gone more than a block or so before I started to feel uncomfortable with my company supplied directions.

The next thing I knew the paved road had turned to gravel and I was quickly looking for a place to turn around. Trying to find a place to turn around your seventy-one feet of heavily loaded tractor trailer in the middle of the night, out in the middle of nowhere in rural Iowa, and on a gravel road is not a comfortable situation for any driver. It is an especially disagreeable circumstance for a driver who has only been out there for several months and has never been faced with anything like this. It is downright disconcerting to say the least. However it does get worse from this point.

I thought I had found what would be a safe spot to turn around. It was not. I managed to get to a spot on the gravel where the ground chose to sink, leaving the back of my trailer in a groundless position. Needless to say I was stuck and no matter what I did at this point, I could not move the truck or trailer.

At this point I was indeed fortunate that my first company had in fact provided me with a working Qualcom unit. In a short time and with the company's assistance, I managed to acquire the help of a local big rig tow operator. They are indeed a welcome sight when you are in such a dire situation.

By this time the sun was starting to come up and traffic was moving about here and there. I managed to attract the attention of some of the locals in the neighborhood and even a local police officer. All these folks were very friendly and tried to assist, but all I really needed was for the tow truck driver to pull me a few feet to get all my wheels back on the gravel.

How could I possibly have ended up in this position? I had followed the directions from the company exactly. The only problem is that they were old directions and directed me down the old highway. The police officer told me that what I actually needed to do was turn down the new highway. My old directions were invariably useless in that regard. This was an embarrassment, but it could have been much worse.

The company paid for the tow truck and I was once again on my way for the last few miles to my delivery point. As luck would have it, on that day I was blessed with very little. Just as I pulled into the driveway of the receiver, and on time as always I might add, my transmission took that moment to die a horrible death. It made sorrowful crunching metal noises as it came to an untimely demise.

I will never know for sure if this had any relation to my previous debacle, but I would guess that it probably did. Either way, I got to the shipper and made the delivery. Another tow vehicle was summoned up on my behalf, at which time we took a nice little ride down to the nearest Freightliner dealer, about 85 miles away in Waterloo. I will never forget Waterloo, Iowa as I spent the next week at the local Motel 6 waiting for a new transmission to be delivered from Pennsylvania.

Unfortunately for me, with my truck in the shop, I had only one option to obtain sustenance. It was the McDonald's across the street from the motel. I eat plenty of stuff from the infamous golden arches, but I usually do so, because it is what I want, not because it is the only game in town. I ate McEverything on the menu, but in reality after several days of this, it became essential to put on the old walking shoes and see the sights of Waterloo. Fortunately, before my feet gave out, I managed to find a small grocery store.

I actually ended up with another nice little relaxing vacation at company expense, but it all came back to one thing. Had I been given accurate directions to my receiver, my company would not have been out the charges for two tow trucks, a new transmission for my Freightliner, a week at Motel 6, and more than likely, to this day I never would have seen the sights of Waterloo, Iowa.

As I have said before, it is almost always up to the driver. You usually end up being responsible for whatever you do. If you are sent down the wrong road due to bad directions, and in turning around you manage to bend the nice metal flanges on the sides of your truck, guess who is at fault? Probably not the company.

I find it quite humorous to observe those flanges on the sides of one particular very large trucking company. I know they deal with a lot of new drivers, but I always wonder how they manage to bend the hell out of so many of their truck flanges. It really is astounding how they don't manage to relay to their drivers, they if you turn the wheel too far, you will have a negative impact on your truck's body. Watch your mirrors!

To make sure you get to the right place most of the time, the first thing you want is a recent copy (no more than a couple years old) of the Trucker Road Atlas. They would like you to purchase a new one every year or so, but once you are out on the road, you see most of the changes and they really aren't too hard to deal with.

If you are going into a big city, there is often a more detailed city map in your Atlas. Try to find your destination on the map. Does it parallel your company directions? If yes try to picture where you are going in advance. Even memorizing your directions and repeating them back to yourself can be helpful. Going to a place with which you are unfamiliar can be difficult enough without trying to read your directions and driving at the same time.

In the event you are fortunate enough to have a computer with you and Internet access, lucky you. Get your own accurate directions off of Yahoo or Map Quest. With an accurate consignee or shipper address you can get where you need to be without relying on your company. The only thing to be cautious of is that not all roads allow big trucks.

Not too long ago, I was involved with a tour going through Chicago. We were storing our trailers just down the road from the event sight. All you had to do was go right up Lakeshore Drive a mile or so and you were there. At least that is what Yahoo would show you. Unfortunately, no trucks are allowed on Lakeshore Drive. We had to go way around the block. It was in reality quite a few miles out of the way. We had to actually go in the opposite direction and through downtown Chicago to get to our event site at the Navy Pier.

Even though Internet directions can be suspect, it is much better to have them than not. In fact if a trucking company spent the few seconds it would take to download those directions and supply them to the drivers, I am convinced it would make a difference, especially for a newer driver who has absolutely no idea where he is going.

Having been the victim of bad directions many more times than I like to think about, I know that corrections in this area would dramatically improve driver retention. What is odd is that companies do not seem to be concerned about it.

In a great many instances, I have observed that the folks in your happy little trucking company office have never set foot inside of a big rig, let alone learned how to drive one. They haven't even a remote clue what is required in its operation. When you suggest they call the company for accurate directions to a facility, they will give you an excuse that "since the people there are not drivers, they probably won't know how to give correct driving directions for a big truck." The truth is they just don't want to take the time to make the call. Laziness rules in your company offices. Bet on it.

In my experience it is sometimes accurate that people don't really know how to direct an 18 wheeler into their facility. But, I would rather have the questionable directions from the mouth of a shipper or receiver, than the certainty of inaccuracies from a buffoon in my trucking company who knows nothing, and in fact has never even been in a truck.

The best bet, if you are not sure where you are going, is to get the shipper or receiver's phone number from your dispatcher and call them yourself. They will tell you to turn right after the convenience store or the fire station. This is certainly a detail that would be ignored by your company representative, who has more interest in getting his next cup of coffee out of the vending machine. It is sometimes amazing how much more accurate are the directions from someone who actually works there.

To be certain you can not rely entirely on directions from

anyone. You are the one that is responsible for getting there. If you are uncertain where your turnoff is located, slow down. If you have to stop, put on your flashers and stop right where you are. It is amazing that when you are in a big rig you do in fact have a bit of extra clout. No one wants you to run over them and they definitely do not want to run into you. They will lose every time.

If you are confused or lost, put those flashers on and stop (but not in the hammer lane of the interstate). Absolutely do not go under the overpass that says height 12'6", when you know your truck is 13'6". This will not be a rewarding experience. Look at many overpasses and you will notice that many people have not heeded the height warnings. Do not let that be you. Having the top of your trailer ripped off is something that will wake you right up, as will the ticket you get for careless driving.

The thing about directions is that you want to go into an area armed with enough knowledge about where you are going to get you through. Many times you will get a big surprise, but you will be able to deal with it if you have planned in advance. If you think you are at the right driveway to turn in to your shipper, but you aren't sure. Put the flashers on, stop, and get out and walk up a little way to be sure. Do not aimlessly take your big rig down a mystery drive only to find out it's not the right one and you can't get back out.

Trust me; it will be a much more comfortable situation for you to get out and get a little exercise rather than to find out too late that you were wrong. Knock on a door and ask if you have to. It is often amazing how helpful people can be, when they realize what you are driving. I think that in general, people are in awe of those that are driving a big truck, because they are terrified of ever doing it themselves.

I know that I am occasionally in awe of myself, when I look at the size of those things. Take a few days off and when you come back you too will be in awe of yourself. You will say, "I can't believe I'm actually driving that huge thing. This is nuts." In actuality there is nothing complicated about it. Just deal with it

.

Off The Road

Off The Road

1. Taking Care Of Business

The most important reason to be a truck driver (professional tourist) is because you are getting paid to do it. Making sure you are in fact getting paid what you are owed is an extra task which you must take on. It is an almost 100% surety that you will sooner or later get shorted by your company. In a very rare situation, you may be over paid for something. However that is as likely as your winning the lottery. So you will have to add accountant to your many talents.

There are numerous ways for drivers to be taken advantage of in regard to their remuneration and you can be assured that your company is well versed in all of them. It is not that they are just trying to rip you off, but if they can avoid paying for something they will. Bet on it. If you don't notice, there is a certainty that they won't either. It is up to you.

Most likely you will have expenses to turn in for reimbursement. You may have toll charges, Cat Scale tickets, faxing or copying charges, and who knows what all. It is up to you to make sure you are paid back for all of your company related expenses. You will need to write down everything you spend and match it up with your pay stubs.

Each time you turn in a receipt you will want to make sure that your name, truck number, trip number, and any other piece of identifying information you can think of is written down on it. Making a copy of your receipts is also not a bad idea as you can count on them to be misplaced by your company. "Did you turn that receipt in? Hmmm, we never received it." You will also need to keep some sort of notebook record of all your expenses, so you can make sure you are getting it all back. Know what to expect when you get paid and then you can charge into the payroll office and let them know that once again they have carelessly ripped you off. Just kidding, but be sure and write it all down.

Judging by the countless times I have been shorted and have had to go through the arduous collection process, I have to guess that companies make veritable millions of dollars each year in funds owed to drivers, that NEVER get paid out. Not all drivers are paying attention to what they are owed and that is their loss. Even doing what I have mentioned to assure payment, you will still very likely end up on the short end occasionally. Always pay attention so that what you are owed matches up with what you get. Do not be intimidated and think you might upset your company by questioning their impeccable accounting practices. You are the one that should be pissed off if they are failing to pay you correctly. By all means if you think you are owed more than you got, SPEAK UP!! They will never come to you and say, "Oh, I think we shorted you $100 last week. Let me cut you a check right now." It will never happen. You snooze. You lose.

Your truck odometer is also a key factor here. Each and every time you stop at a receiver, shipper, truck stop, your girl friend's house (uh, skip that one), or pretty much anywhere, you need to make a habit of taking an odometer reading. Keep track of all your miles. If you drive from Denver, Colorado to Ontario, California and it takes you 982 miles, and your company only pays you for 880, by all means speak up to the company.

Chances are good that you will get shorted on your miles, because as your company will probably tell you, they don't pay for city miles. This sucks! In other words you may have to drive through a hellacious two hour traffic jam in Los Angeles only to be shorted by your company because they won't pay you a few extra dollars. Not all companies do this, but in my experience most do. Why they can do this, I'm not sure other than it is just something they all have always gotten away with, and until all the drivers stand up for their rights it will continue. Drivers standing up for their rights? That will happen soon, uhhh, like never.

When I started driving, I was told to expect to be shorted ten percent on all the miles I drove. In most cases that has proven to be relatively accurate. What this means is, if you were supposedly being paid 30 cents per mile, in reality you may only be making 27 cents per mile. This is one of the realities of rip off in the trucking industry. Drivers being short changed on payment for miles driven most definitely contributes to the ridiculously high employment turnover rate in the transportation industry. Add it up over a years' time and it can be thousands of dollars per driver. Guess who pockets that change?

Even though the likelihood of your being paid for all your miles is limited at best, it is never wrong to ask about it. By all means complain that you want to be paid for those extra hours you spent sitting, on behalf of your company, in that construction zone twenty mile traffic backup in downtown Los Angeles. You want to be paid for the extra 102 miles you had to drive from Denver to Ontario. There was no other way to go and those were the miles you were required to drive to get there. "I want my money!"

The more drivers that are willing to voice their dissatisfaction about being shorted, the more likely a company is to take notice. And, be assured, that your dispatchers, driver managers, and the like do have the authorization to throw you an occasional bone. They can give you money. If they say otherwise, they are either lying or the company thinks as little of them as the do their drivers.

If you want to get paid you will have to let them know that you are owed. You have nothing to lose by asking and everything to gain. The worst thing that will happen is that they will say "no." They are not going to fire you for asking. The only reason you are there is to get paid and they know it. You will not offend them by asking and may in fact gain some respect for speaking up on your behalf. But, if you say nothing, you will receive nothing in return.

In spite of the fact that you are likely to be cheated out of pay for the city miles, you may in fact just have been shorted by a miscalculation by your payroll department. These are not CPA's doing this and even though payroll is not an especially complicated process, they will frequently make mistakes. And as I said, it will very rarely be in your favor. Know what you are owed and make sure you get it!

I have always been willing to complain if I am owed. One time I was shorted on a reimbursement for a reweigh ticket from a Cat Scale. They paid me for the original $8 scale ticket, but did not give me that extra dollar, that I took out of my pocket to reweigh their overloaded merchandise. Conveniently they didn't have the receipt, which I had turned in with the original. They paid me my dollar. Had I not asked, I would have paid for the reweigh myself, right along with all the time I had spent driving around to get their overloaded merchandise reloaded.

In my experience of complaining about money owed, most of the time it has been beneficial. I have frequently collected extra money for miles driven and not paid for. Many times I have gotten extra delay pay for the wasted seven hours or so, that I have spent sitting at some loading dock waiting on some cretin to take the twenty minutes it actually takes to put the twenty pallets on the back of my trailer. These people are paid by the hour and could not care less how long you have to sit waiting in the back of your truck.

You are paid for driving and not for sitting around endlessly waiting. Usually your company has a policy of some sort in regard to those circumstances, but they will not come right out and offer you money for your valuable time. If you don't care enough to speak up, then you do not deserve to be compensated.

If your truck breaks down and you need a hotel because you can't sleep in the truck. Tell them immediately. They are likely not to care that it is 95 degrees outside and you have no air conditioning. It will be much warmer in the truck with the blazing sun heating up the inside to unbearable temperatures. They do not care. They are sitting in their comfortable little office chair, in a comfortably air conditioned office, sipping on their Starbucks, and showing no concern whatsoever for any driver welfare or discomfort.

You need to be put up in the local hotel now and if you have to put out your own money in advance for that, make sure you are reimbursed for every penny. I have had just such occurrences on more than one occasion and the company has conveniently forgotten to pay me back even though they got my receipts. Speak up and get paid.

I would say that most companies underestimate the basic intellect of the average driver by figuring they can get away with regularly taking advantage of them. However, in my experience it is rare to see drivers that are willing to speak up on their own behalf in regard to being shortchanged. Thus I don't really think they have been intellectually underestimated. If you are going to be a sucker, then you shall be treated as such. That great showman P. T. Barnum said, "There's a sucker born every minute." No doubt that plenty of them are now driving big rigs. And of course W. C. Fields made that classic comedy, "Never Give a Sucker an Even Break." That pretty much says it all and be assured that trucking companies are taking it to heart and getting away with it. Ask and receive!

<u>Off The Road</u>

2. Getting Loaded, Unloaded, & Wasting Time

One of the most negative things in the life of a "professional tourist" is the ridiculous amount of wasted time sitting around at a shipper for hours and hours waiting for some poor warehouse worker to take the 20 minutes that is actually required to load or unload your trailer. If you are someone with little patience (I am), it can be unbearable (And, it is).

Too many times I have been told to go to some shipper and pick up a pre-loaded trailer. "It is ready to go now. They are waiting for you to get there." Upon arrival I am informed that, "Well, uhh, we didn't have no empties so we couldn't uhh get it loaded." Excuses are rampant and in fact ever present in the transportation biz.

There is an excuse for every damn thing imaginable and yet the ONLY thing that matters here is that it is the driver that pays for it. The morons in your company rarely give a damn and the company you are waiting at also could not care any less that you have to wait for 8 or 9 or 10 straight hours, or even longer. THEY DO NOT CARE! What is bad about this is that you do not get paid for sitting around. You only get paid for driving, unless you follow instructions from the previous section.

It is possible that your company will occasionally reimburse you for your time. It is called delay pay. However, getting it is often akin to pulling teeth. There is a strong possibility that your company will find all kinds of excuses why they are not going to pay you for your delay. Count on it. They are not going to come right out and say, "That was horrible making you sit around all that time. So, we are going to pay you an extra $200 for your time." This is not a likely scenario. If you expect to get paid anything for your time, you will have to ask and sometimes ask repeatedly.

Not only will it be likely that you will not be paid, they may even berate you for idling your engine for the air conditioning comfort that you got during that time. After all it was only 98 degrees in the shade and without the AC it could be 125 degrees in your truck. The fact that you sat there all day cost you the big money you could have made going down the highway. The moron loading your trailer does not care about your wait, because he is getting paid by the hour.

The point here is that if in fact you are required to wait endlessly for someone else to do their job, and it will happen with regularity, you want to be doing something useful. That could be one of any number of things.

Doing the most productive thing possible at all times while waiting is essential to your maintenance of sanity while on the road. It could be as simple as sleeping while waiting to get loaded, because you intend to drive all night to your destination. If you have had plenty of sleep maybe you can clean up inside your truck or do your daily inspection. Do something useful.

If you know you will be waiting for awhile, you can always walk up the street to your favorite fast food establishment and devour mass quantities of very delicious artery cloggers. Eat when you get a chance, as you may not have the time later or an ability to find parking at the truck stop.

You might just walk to the local mall and go shopping. When you sit in a truck all the time, you will be lacking in the exercise department. If the mall is a mile up the road, so what. One mile there and one mile back. A good brisk walk will be good for you and help to clear those diesel fume cobwebs out of your brain. Yes in case you didn't know it, you are in fact sucking plenty of those noxious potentially cancer causing diesel fumes up into your lungs and it ain't healthy. Take that to the bank.

Take note at the local truck stop and see how many male truck drivers appear to be nine months pregnant and about to give birth at any moment. Are you one of them? Many drivers are seriously out of shape. And if you are one of them get out of the truck frequently and walk a few miles. It only takes a few minutes to get warmed up and get your blood pumping through the veins, but it is good for you. Do it often enough and it will become a habit. Just sit around in your truck and soon you will look exactly like the rest of the lazy unhealthy truck drivers with the massive protruding guts.

Not long ago one of the drivers from a company I was with had a delivery in Union City, California. This is basically an outer suburb of Oakland, and driving there can be a very tense and life threatening experience by itself. His trailer was unloaded and when he failed to pull his rig from the dock, someone from the company came out to let him know there were other drivers waiting for his spot. To their surprise this driver did not respond to their banging on the side of his truck. Alas this poor fellow had had a heart attack and expired right in his cab.

Who knows what was really wrong with this guy? Maybe this would have happened anyway, but it is a certainty that if you don't get out and burn up a few calories, it will come back to haunt you eventually.

Driving can be a very stressful situation. Driving around in a big truck in a big metropolitan area such as Oakland can kill you. Get some exercise and stay away from the "all you can eat" buffets at the truck stop. Generally they are a little less than tasty anyway.

If you are stuck in your cab waiting, there are a lot of things you can do. There are drivers with very elaborate video, television, and stereo set-ups connected to satellites and all kinds of things. I am not that serious about it. I have a nice little $15 black and white TV that invariably picks up at least one local station right off the air waves in pretty much any town I am in. It is really all you need and I never worry about someone breaking in and stealing it. Those things can also happen.

Some drivers have their bicycle attached to the back of their truck. Go for a ride and see the sights. Aside from getting paid, that is why you are in this business anyway. Bring your guitar along and practice while waiting. Work on your tax return. Read a book or newspaper. There are a thousand different things with which you might occupy your down time.

If nothing else pick up one of those many free magazines you grabbed while walking out of the truck stop. You know, the ones that have all the truck companies that are begging for drivers, and tell you how they are the best and they will pay you more than anyone else. This way you will have a small idea of who is out there looking for you once you get your first year of experience.

On top of it all, if you think you have been waiting an unreasonably long time, call your company, complain loudly, and let them know you will never again come to this place. Then get your lazy ass in to that inconsiderate facility and ask those mindless buffoons "what is taking so long!" If you just sit there and say nothing, they won't mind. They will also take as long as they like to get you loaded or emptied. This is often another one of those "up to you" situations, that you had better deal with, or prepare to absorb the consequences.

Just don't waste too much of your time. It is all valuable and you can't get it back after it is gone. Life is way too short to spend much time sitting at grocery warehouses.

<u>Off The Road</u>

3. Hanging Out At The Truck Stop, OR
How To Spend Your Money Fast

The truck stop can be a desert oasis out in the middle of nowhere, or it can be vacuum sucking all the money out of your wallet. Be forewarned that the bargains are few and far between and you better get there early if you expect to get a parking place. The showering facilities are often lacking and even downright filthy. High levels of bacteria are ever present in the food if not actual food poisoning. The service in the restaurants very likely will be poor at best. The parking lots reek from the stench of urine of brain dead truck drivers who were unable to find the bathroom or more likely just didn't care. This is just a reality of every day trucker life.

That being said, it is only a generality and while most frequent, it is not always the case. I have always been able to find a parking spot at the world's largest truck stop in Walcott, Iowa and their showers are always cleaned properly. Occasionally the service and food in a few truck stop restaurants is above reproach. It doesn't happen often.

Some truck stops charge nine bucks for a shower, but since you are a frequent fueler, with a frequent fueler card, you are entitled to a free shower every time you fuel up. And after you have been on the road for several showerless days, running water of any kind looks inviting. Generally, even though the management will say, "Our showers are well cleaned and disinfected after every use," they are lying bastards. Too often I have watched the professional shower cleaners as I wait my turn. They can walk into a shower room, grab a dirty towel and replace it, run an already filthy germ infested nasty mop across the floor, and be out of there in less than twenty seconds.

Not to cast aspersions upon the credibility of a professional shower cleaner, because NOBODY wants that job, but I always feel an obligation to keep my shoes on when taking a shower as opposed to walking on a potentially disease ridden floor. Alright it's usually not that bad, but damn near. Do you really think they change the mop water regularly? Hmmm.

Now that you have showered up and are all nice and clean, it is time to eat. It is also time to examine your options of where to eat. I have probably walked out of more truck stop restaurants and fast food franchises than I have eaten in. Too often the people that work there appear to be unkempt transient deadbeats. If the employees look like that, just imagine the amount of pride they take in preparing the meal, that you will soon devour in to your digestive tract.

Look at the floor in these places. Is it clean? Or does it appear neglected, as in there are leftover French fries all over the floor, spilt coffee stains, and who knows what all in various stages of mold or decay on the walls and seats. Are there flies all over the windows? You know what flies are attracted to? Rotting food and fecal matter. Observe such things and just imagine what the kitchen, that you can't see, looks like. These are signals to let you know, that this is the place to avoid. Leave immediately or pay the consequences.

Too often, you will be driving down the road, having eaten a couple hours ago, at one of the aforementioned facilities, only to notice a strangely uncomfortable feeling in your stomach. Soon after it will become undeniably apparent to you of the immediate necessity of the procurement of a bathroom facility. It will be the one and only priority on your list of things to do NOW! Nothing else will matter!

I can not tell you how important it is to your sense of well being to carry with you a package of happy little anti-diarrhea pills. In all the years that I have cooked things for myself, I have never once had the infamous "got to go now" attack and yet when you hit the road, it is once again about a 100% certainty that it will happen and with regularity if you are not careful.

It is not just truck stop restaurants to watch out for. This will happen even in the best known fast food establishments. You name 'em and it happens there too. EVERY ONE OF THEM! Having previously owned and operated a full service restaurant and night club, I can speak with authority on this subject. Too often the people that work in these places do not care about what you put into your digestive tract. It is strictly up to you to make such decisions. You best choose wisely or you will inevitably suffer the consequences of your poor judgment

I swear that like clockwork, when I sit down to eat in nearly any fast food chain, they either immediately come out with a mop, or a spray bottle of some sort of vile smelling spray cleaner in order to show what an effort they make to keep the place clean. How do you like your ammonia spray and dirty mop water when you are about to eat? "Ahh, nothing like some fresh bleach water to go with your super-sized cheese burger." They just don't get it and they just don't care. Many of these people that work there are either high school kids on their first job or people that can't find a real job elsewhere. Trust me; they do not have even the slightest concern whether or not they are spraying ammonia cleaner on your tacos.

I have watched these same people, from where I am

sitting, walk into the bathroom and mop the floor. They then proceed to mop the floor of their restaurant with the same mop and water, that they just used to clean the urine soaked and fecal matter stained bathroom. How often do you suppose they actually change this mop and water?

Do you think they have any regard for what some truck driver is eating. They are just performing a menial task that they have been assigned. If the hamburger has been sitting out for several hours acquiring bacteria and fly feces, who cares? You better!

You have to be observant of everything when you are on the road. I prefer to eat in places where the workers are middle aged women, that look like your mother or sister, or even somebody's grandmother. These folks tend to keep a clean and health conscious facility. They appear to have pride in what they are doing and I have never had a problem in such places.

Another good place to eat is the one in which you see quite a few senior citizens in attendance. Make no mistake about it. With age occasionally also comes wisdom. These folks know where to go and are not eating here for the "$8.95 All You Can Eat Salmonella Special."

Wherever you choose to eat, be sure you are comfortable, with who is making the food you are putting into your digestive system. Do they wash their hands? Do they use those required plastic gloves before handling something you will eventually put in your mouth? Once you have experienced a few personal difficulties, you will notice this with "regularity." Pun intended.

I can't over emphasize this, because no matter what you do and how carefully you choose where you will eat, the evil demon of digestive destruction will eventually come to call. "If you are in doubt, you must walk out." Damn, another poem. I am on a roll. There is nearly always another fast food place in close proximity to where you are. You might have to walk a block or two. If not, that is why you keep a good supply of emergency food in your truck. Right?

Another word on eating. The "all you can eat buffet" is often the cheapest way to go and yet you might be better off with something right off the menu. You never really know how many days that salad dressing has been sitting around. "Uhhh, just stir it up a little and they'll never notice the mold. It's good for at least a couple more days." Also, if you are tempted to eat "all you can eat" you may regret that later on too. More is not necessarily better. Moderation is the key here.

Some of the buffets are not too bad, but too often it just tastes like something that has been sitting in a pan too long and is overcooked and over heated. It is either tasteless or just doesn't taste that good. If after checking it out, there is any doubt, skip it.

Also consider, that when you actually go into a restaurant to sit down and order off a menu from a "professional" server, you should expect quality service. If they treat you like they are doing you a favor, take 45 minutes to bring you a simple hamburger, screw up the order, and then expect you to tip them 20%, there are alternatives. Those happy little fast food restaurants are usually going to provide you with superior service, equivalent food products, and do it for less than half the price of those overrated, over priced, full service establishments. It is of course up to you to make the final determination of where and what you choose to eat. Make your choices wisely.

Now that you have consumed mass quantities of artery clogging delicacies, it is time to entertain yourself. Numerous truck stops have an infamous game room, filled with fun little video distractions. I have observed drivers that sit in these game rooms hour after hour, depositing large amounts of change, and amusing themselves. I have never put money into any of these. If that is what you enjoy, then by all means spend your money. To me it is a waste. You are out on the road trying to make money, not blow it on a silly video game.

Some of these games even simulate Las Vegas casino slot machines, but they do not pay out money. Do not be a moron. If you want to play casino games, go to Las Vegas or Reno, where you actually have a small chance of getting something back. If you are on the road for a bit, there is a high probability that you will get a chance to stop at a real gambling facility. They are everywhere and they often cater to truck drivers. Do not accept a substitute. Even though you still won't get much back, the real thing is much more entertaining. Bet on it!

Most "real" truck stops have some sort of TV room, which either has cable access or plays non-stop videos of your favorite adventure flicks. This is free and can certainly kill a bit of time. The only negative here is you will often be surrounded by numerous other drivers or other folks. Some of the people in there can be of questionable repute. They can smell like a rotting garbage dump or reek of cigarette smoke. In fact I occasionally wonder if these are sometimes homeless street bums, not actual drivers, and just looking for a place to spend the night.

You will indeed encounter numerous strange folks at ye olde truck stop. You will frequently have some guy come up to you saying "I'm a driver and I just need ten more dollars to get home to Nacogdoches. If you could just help me out a little I'd really preciate it." Do not help him out! Do not give him money! He is not going to Nacogdoches. And, above all, do not offer this person a ride anywhere, ever! There is probably a one in a thousand chance that he is telling the truth, and a 99.9% chance that he is a lying dirt bag!

It is not only a guy who will do this. You will get some pathetic little teenage girl coming up to you with a similarly sad and depressing tale of woe and despair. I usually suggest that they call their parents and ask them for assistance, or maybe some similar solution.

You can not get involved in everybody's troubles or you will soon develop your own. Avoid these folks or pay the consequences. The best answer is going to be, "Not interested," and walk briskly away. You may feel guilty, but not for long. Trust me when I suggest aggressive avoidance in all such situations.

Inevitably you will come across that well known anomaly the "lot lizard." This is a must to avoid and yet every day some truckers make the choice to get "involved." A "lot lizard" is a prostitute, a potentially disease laden bar tramp, that is more than willing to assist you in a departure from your cash reserves.

More than likely your initial confrontation will be by a little knock on your truck door, and usually when you are sleeping. You may be at the truck stop. You may just be parked in a rest area at the side of the highway. It can happen anywhere and everywhere. You may even be confronted as you walk through a truck stop, but make no mistake about it, it will happen eventually and your response should always be the same. "No thanks."

I was parked at a truck stop a day early for my delivery in Birmingham, Alabama. It was raining hard and I was very tired from a long drive. In the 24 hour period, that I sat there, I received four separate knocks on the door, from four separate young "ladies." They were all looking to help me part ways with my meager cash holdings.

It has happened numerous other times. You can deal with such eventualities as you wish. Just keep in mind, it is illegal and you can have your rig impounded and be hauled off to jail as a common criminal. And all you wanted to do was "hang with a ho." My advice, once again is to just say, "No thanks. Not interested."

Aside from the obvious, you also don't know what they really want. Maybe their cohorts are hiding at the back of your trailer and waiting to rob you personally. Perhaps they are just interested in that trailer full of big screen high definition plasma TV's you are hauling across the country. You just never really know. Do you?

The only logical option here is aggressive avoidance. I don't care how good it looks. You do not want to get involved, unless you are willing to suffer the consequences of foolish indiscretion.

As I have said, there are relatively few bargains to be had at the truck stop. It is often better to wait for the opportunity to stock up on necessities until you get to the local Wal Mart or some other such discount facility. Occasionally though there are a few bargains. Often the truck stops are trying to unload last years laminated Trucker Road Atlas at 90% off. Feel free to snag one or two. They can actually be good for quite a few years.

Sometimes you can get something cheap that they over bought and are now trying to unload, but in general truck stop merchandise is for your convenience only and it is usually more than fully priced. And, when you see that pre-made sandwich, normally overpriced at a rip off $3.99, now at a bargain basement half off $1.99, bet money that it should have been gracing the dumpster in back of the facility several days prior. Avoid! Avoid! Avoid!

One further note in regard to the major truck stops (TA, Flying J, Petro, Pilot, etc.). A nice little benefit is supplied to frequent fuelers. Unless you are an owner/operator looking for the cheapest fuel, it is a nice little dividend for a company driver. For each gallon of fuel you buy, you get a penny bonus added to your Frequent Fueler Card (Don't forget to sign up for all of them). It doesn't really seem like much, but it does add up. Occasionally one of those franchises has bonus months, where they actually offer two cents a gallon.

You can waste fuel bonuses by getting an occasional free meal at the restaurant or you can do like I do and save it up for something more desirable at the truck stop store. I confess to having gotten numerous free items with my Frequent Fueler Points, including 2 CB's, a police scanner, a large air mattress and rechargeable compressor pump, a briefcase, a knife, and even a happenin' little shiny blue electric scooter, that to this day sits in my storage unit waiting to be ridden or sold.

I've gotten quite a bit of other free stuff, but this is what comes to mind. Currently I have well over $300 on my TA Frequent Fueler card. Just hoping something I want will pop up soon. Eventually you have to spend it, but it might as well be for something useful. It's a nice little bonus and all you have to do is spend your company's money fueling up. Nothing to complain about with this nice little program.

The hardest thing about truck stops is usually just being able to get in them and get a parking spot. As I have said elsewhere, the best time to get a spot is generally early in the morning, when many drivers are pulling out to tend to their day's business. The worst time is usually in the evening when all the good spots are full and will remain so for the rest of the night. In many larger cities, the only place to go with a big rig is to the only truck stop in the area. Very often these places are jam packed by mid afternoon, leaving many drivers wondering where they will go now.

The inability to secure parking can be one of the worst experiences for a driver and especially for a rookie. Drivers that have been around a few years very often know of other available parking in places that a beginner would never imagine. There are usually spots, even if you have to park somewhere on some back street for the night, but if you are completely unfamiliar with the area, you may be out of luck. It has definitely happened to me and more than a few times.

The best bet is to plan your arrival time to coincide with your ability to obtain a parking spot at the truck stop, where you will have access to those essential things like food, showers, bath rooms, laundry facilities, pay phones. If you have to drive a few extra hours to get there at the appropriate time, then do so and avoid complications later.

When you have just driven half way across the country it is so much easier to just pull right in to a nice big parking spot, that is right outside the main entrance door of the truck stop. When you are really tired is not the best of all times to attempt a negotiation of a barely big enough for a mini bike spot right in between two $150k Peterbilts.

You do not want to knock somebody's mirror off, or scrape their bumper just because you have been driving all day and are exhausted. This is not a good idea. You want to arrive at the best time for you to secure a good spot. If you can get there by early afternoon, then good for you. It never works for me. I always seem to be driving by the truck stops at night and noticing all the drivers there getting their ten hours off, as I keep on rollin' along down the highway. However it works for you, if you plan ahead you will be rewarded.

Enough about truck stops. You will inevitably figure it all out. As I have said, nothing here is complicated. You just need to develop your routine and it will become comfortable for you.

Odds And Ends

Odds And Ends

1. Watch Those Mirrors

There are a few loose ends that require elaboration and this is where we will discuss them. They are mostly things you should learn about in truck school, with your new company, or even both, but they are worthy of mention here also. They are things that require repetition if only because they are safety issues.

It is hard to say enough about mirrors. When you drive a big truck, you can't just look out the back window and see what is going on behind you. Usually there is no back window, but even if there was it wouldn't matter. If you are hooked to a 53 foot trailer you won't be enjoying much of a view anyway. You have to get used to using your mirrors. Your mirrors can save your life.

Always make sure they are adjusted properly and cleaned so that you can see what is going on around you. No matter how perfect you get them, there will always be that happy little goofball in the mini van who will manage to sneak into that one spot you can not see in your mirrors. You have to watch constantly for these people. They are blissfully and completely unaware that you can't see them and will invariably sit there in your blind spot waiting for you to crush them into a pile of scrap metal.

Especially watch out for the dark green mini van operators. I believe that somewhere along the way these folks have received special training in the proper protocol for irritation of truck drivers. While they often do appear as candidates to be squashed like a bug, I suggest that you really do not want that on your conscience.

So much is happening around you that you must be aware of the mirrors at all times. It can not be stressed enough that you will have to deal with this every day on the highway. Other trucks are going to come up on you going twice your speed. You need to be watching for this.

When you are on a windy mountain road and very cautiously going twenty miles an hour, I may even be coming up behind you in my racing truck and sailing by (I love windy mountain roads). Cars and trucks appear out of nowhere from behind you. Watch those mirrors dammit!

Probably more minor accidents happen because of truck drivers not using their mirrors properly, not just driving, but when backing up into a loading dock or even just a parking place. Keep in mind though that even proper use of those mirrors won't always avoid problems. If there is any doubt whatsoever, about what is behind you, GET OUT AND LOOK!!

Do not be a lazy driver. Mirrors are also deceptive. When you fail to get your lazy ass out of the truck to look, and you back into the goofball that just parked his brand new SUV right directly behind you, where you could not possibly see him even with your perfectly adjusted shiny clean mirrors, it will be your fault and you will pay for it. Just because some idiot was stupid enough to pull right in back of where you were about to back up (it does happen), you will still be the guilty party if you backed into his car. I know this because not long ago a driver I was talking to had just performed this act on somebody's brand new SUV and he was in fact the responsible party.

As I say often, truck drivers rarely get enough exercise. Spend a few of those inexpensively acquired calories that you have accumulated at the ever present "all you can eat" buffet, and climb from your cab to the ground to see how much room you actually have before you back into the side of that $150,000 new Peterbilt, or that concrete wall that looks to be way off in the distance. You have plenty of room until you don't. Get out and look and avoid future complications. Enough about mirrors.

Sometimes you have to make it fit even without enough room. There is definitely not 71 feet here, but you have to keep a happy customer.

Getting into this spot was a virtual impossibility. You had to maneuver backwards around the corner. The drive straight ahead was not useable except as an exit. Judging by the substantial brick damage to the surrounding buildings, not everyone has had success at this facility.

<u>Odds And Ends</u>

2. Chains, Snow, & Ice - Aggressive Avoidance

Another point of major driver irritation comes in the form of tire chains. Many drivers have never even seen them, but if you travel to places like California, between November and April, you are required to carry them. You can at times there be required to put chains on all eight of your drive tires. This can be a horrendous experience. Other places, like Vail Pass and the Eisenhower Tunnel in Colorado may only require you to put chains on four of the drive tires.

When you drive around the country in the winter, you need to be prepared for all potential disasters. For me, being told that I must put chains on, if I want to continue driving on the road, is a disaster. Driving in the mountains in the winter time, it can snow at almost any time and anywhere, and when the sign says "chains required," they mean it. Tickets for this are costly for getting caught without the chains on, and even more expensive if you get stuck and impede the flow of traffic due to your chain negligence.

Drivers in the eastern half of the United States are less likely to deal with this, but when you get to the mountains out west, it is something you must always be aware of. Many drivers will say that, "If the weather is bad enough, that chains are required, you should not be out on the road anyway." I don't disagree with that; I just don't want to put those lousy chains on at all.

Once you know how to do it and you have done it a few times, maybe it gets to be a part of your routine. Not for me! Chains are nasty, greasy, road filth covered hunks of very heavy metal. When they get wet and you pick them up, it is a guarantee that you will get that greasy sludge all over yourself and your clothes. It does not come out in the wash and just trying to get it off your hands is a monumental task. And of course, when you are out on a mountain highway in the middle of a snowstorm, you are certain to have access to cleaning facilities. Right?

There you are sitting in your nice warm truck and all of a sudden you are expected to get out into the blowing wet snow in minus 10 degrees and play professional chain dude. NOT FOR ME! I have performed this act twice and barring very unforeseen circumstances beyond my control, it will never happen again.

The first time I put the chains on was only a few months after I had started driving big trucks. It was at Vail Pass in Colorado. I got out of the truck at the chain up area on the east bound side of Interstate 70 and got right on it. I had brand new chains so they were less likely to provide me with access to the grimy filth associated with the well worn variety of used tire chains. I spent about a half hour "chaining up" and was ready to get back on the icy highways of Colorado.

I think I may have gotten almost ten or twelve yards up the highway before my brand new tire chains unhooked from the tires and fell off. Fortunately, I was still well within the confines of the chain up area, and thus was blessed with the opportunity to further hone my mastery of chain-up skills. Needless to say I did not get it right the first time and was not looking forward with enthusiasm and excitement towards my second opportunity to perform this task.

When I had been given my set of brand new chains, I had been told by the company to throw away my old style cables, that had been previously used in the chain up process by someone else in this truck. Fortunately I hold the title of master pack rat and am unwilling to throw much of anything away. I put my nice set of new chains back in the truck and proceeded to drag out the old cables. I figured I had little to lose. I could not possibly have any less luck, than I had had with the others. I was right.

After another battle with the ice, snow, and road grime on my cables (which was now pretty much road grime all over me and my clothes), I was once again ready to head on down the Interstate. This time I was successful. To this day no one has ever really instructed me in the fine art of chaining up, so I was definitely on my own here.

I somehow have come to believe, that since no company has ever made even the slightest attempt at inquiry to find out if I have even a remote clue in regard to putting chains on, that just maybe they don't really want or expect drivers to do so. I don't think they would try to force anyone to put them on, but things like the U.S. Mail certainly must go through in all kinds of inclement weather.

There are places where there actually are people for hire, that will chain you up. I'm not paying for that and your company will probably also balk at such an opportunity.

With my newly attached cables I managed to sail up and over the Vail Pass and was equally successful getting up to and through the Eisenhower Tunnel. I had done it and could now pull over and remove the chains (errr, uhhh, cables). However my hands and feet were still frozen numb from my previous endeavors and I was hesitant to once again exit the vehicle. So, I didn't.

As I approached the weigh station that is almost perennially open and just a few miles east of the Eisenhower Tunnel, I thought to myself, that they may want to know why I had yet to remove my happy little cables. I don't really know if they would have questioned me, but this was not really something to look forward to.

As I thought about this, a miracle occurred. Magically those cables (that my company had told me to dispose of anyway in the terminal dumpster), chose that exact moment to disconnect from my drive wheels and trail off into a snow bank at the side of the road. This was a truly remarkable occurrence and a timely fate indeed for those evil demon cables. As I had been told to throw them out, I felt absolutely no desire whatsoever to go back and retrieve them. I didn't. They had served their purpose well and were to be used by me, "Nevermore."

I will say that in many miles of driving through raging snow and ice storms, I never again have chained up. I have since driven under completely absurd icy and snow packed conditions where the only things that kept me from going over the cliff were the rumble strips at the side of the road.

I have kept going sometimes just because it was snowing so hard that the road signs, mile markers, and highway exits were obliterated by the wind and snow. The ice balls that form between your windshield and your wipers keep the two several inches apart and make seeing out the front a virtual impossibility.

I have driven over some ridiculous mountain roads, because I wanted to get somewhere, and yet I have never once had my truck or trailer go sideways on me. Never! Kill me, but I have never slid on the ice in my truck. Blind luck? Maybe, or maybe not.

Sometimes you have little choice, but to keep going. If you can't see the exit ramps, mile markers, or road signs, and basically have no idea where the hell you are, or if you should even try to get off at some visible exit, it could be in your best interest to keep going. It is not snowing everywhere, and maybe too often I have kept going until the roads were dry. Either way, I have always managed to come out unscathed and with truck and trailer intact.

I have seen many, many trucks that have managed to slide into each other or just by themselves go right off an icy road. Under such circumstances you best learn quickly that slower is better. You keep both hands on the wheel (not on your cigarette, cell phone, CB, cup of coffee, or any other damn thing that you will later try and use as an excuse for an accident), both eyes on the road ahead of you, and do not make any sudden erratic moves.

You can dramatically increase your odds of successfully maneuvering through a major blizzard and sheet ice roads by being cautious. It does require 100% concentration and just because you are very tired is not relevant. If there is nowhere to get off the road, you keep going and keep focused on keeping your tractor and trailer straight. You just take it slow and easy.

Make no mistake about it; as much as I enjoy driving, I hate snow. If you can avoid it, do so. Sometimes, you just run right into it and are forced to comply with nature. When left with no alternatives, you deal with it.

I ran into just such a situation only a few months after I started driving. Many unusual incidents will take place within your first few months on the highway. I was headed west on Interstate 40 and was in New Mexico just west of Albuquerque. Within only a few miles, the weather turned from sunny with dry roads, to rain, to snow, and then to raging blizzard conditions with a road of sheet ice. Upon careful reflection, I was already days ahead on this load, and probably should have stayed where I was just a few hours before in Amarillo, Texas.

Not knowing what was ahead I just watched the road

carefully and kept on going. As I came over the top of a hill, and what a surprise to see, there were trucks crashed everywhere. They were mostly on the eastbound side and the road straight ahead of me was still passable. As I said there was nowhere to stop, so you either kept moving or you could slide right off the road and crash into whatever stopped you.

There was one car left on the road in front of me and I think he panicked, when he saw all the wrecks. I watched as he slid right off the highway into a big hole in the median. He wasn't hurt, but he was stuck.

There are rules that say you are supposed to stop at all wrecks and render any possible assistance. However, there are also rules of self preservation. When there is absolutely nowhere to pull over without causing further accidents, "discretion becomes the better part of valor." It would have been foolish and very dangerous to do anything but keep on trying to get through.

There was no question that numerous vehicles were wrecked all over the road at that time and I had nothing to lose. If I had crashed I had a great excuse. I could say, "Everyone else crashed and so did I." However, I did not crash. I continued on through the blinding snow, wind, and ice. My wipers had those big thick ice balls stuck between them and the windshield, so looking out the front window was not much of an option. I stuck my head out the window and attempted to follow tracks on the road, that had been left by previous drivers. Unfortunately, those tracks soon disappeared and I found myself to be completely alone heading west on Interstate 40.

They had in fact shut down the whole interstate and probably just seconds after I passed through. I was now on my own and all by myself. As absurd as this was to be out on the highway in this disastrous storm, there was now no other choice. I was in the middle of it and had to keep on rolling. I was already very tired when I ran into this storm, but now concentration became essential. Driving on for another hour or two (not sure exactly, because when you are in the middle of such things, time really does stand still), I managed to get to Albuquerque, where there was in fact no snow and the roads were dry. What a relief.

As it turned out, this ended up on the national news, and apparently thirteen people were killed in that massive wreck. They were in a van that was crushed by a big rig. It must have been on the eastbound side and I am glad to have avoided it. As I said before, I hate driving in snow. The only thing worse is driving in snow and then being told you must put on the chains to continue. On now to other subjects of relevance.

<u>Odds And Ends</u>

3. Hot Brakes

Have you ever noticed those "runaway truck ramps," usually along the highway as you are going down a mountain hill? Not very often do you see anything going on there, but they are there for a reason. The reason being that when a tractor trailer operator has lost his brakes and can't stop, he can pull into the deep sands of the safety ramp. Such things can save your life.

The point here is that in most cases the use of those facilities can be avoided. The reason that the brakes go out in a truck is generally from over use. They are supposed to teach you in truck school, that when you are hauling 45,000 lbs of bottled water and you are flying down a 6% mountain grade, your truck will just go faster and faster. You of course will feel the need to keep applying the brakes harder and harder.

The only problem with using the brakes over and over is that they start to heat up. When they get really hot you will notice the vile stench of something on the order of burning electrical wire. The first time you notice the odor you will know what it is. It is like seeing your first rattle snake. There will be little doubt that that is what it is. There may be a doubt as to who it is. Many trucks over use their brakes, when going down a hill.

If you are a careful driver you will most likely still be visited frequently with the fresh odor of the burning brakes. While you may be initially alarmed, you will also realize that you have been careful with your brakes and the problem is actually that of other drivers.

When you keep on over using the brakes, you will soon notice smoke coming from your rig. If you have allowed it to get to this point, you best act quickly. Your brakes are over heating and could be nearing the point of being non-functional.

Once the brakes get too hot, aside from that nice burning smell and smoke, you will notice that you no longer have working brakes. In this case you can look for the runaway truck ramp or maybe just a large group of 4 wheelers to run over and cushion your truck as it crashes, rolls over and explodes in a ball of flames. Or, not!

This is a situation in which you never want to find yourself. But, no matter how many times it is drilled into your brain, there is a certain segment of the truck driving populace that will ignore all warnings, and drive their brakeless death machines right into the side of a mountain or an unsuspecting motorist.

The trick is to not ever get your brakes into overheating mode. You are often warned by the road signs of an impending down grade. If you are hauling a heavy load, you are first of all going to shift down into a lower gear and then you are going to use your happy little engine brake.

The engine brake (sometimes called a Jake brake) is that usually noisy low pitched growling engine sound that scares the hell out of you when you are driving your car down the highway in the presence of big trucks. It slows down a truck without ever touching the real brakes.

Shifting into a lower gear also slows down the truck. Additionally, you will want to perform your downshifting task prior to heading down the hill. If you don't, you may find it difficult if not impossible to shift once you are flying down the mountain.

These are the tools that you will learn to use with

regularity on a mountain road in order to avoid that nice smell of your overheated burning brakes and any necessity to utilize the runaway truck ramp. Keep in mind also that once you use the runaway ramp, someone will have to come and pull you out. Those deep sands are there for a good purpose and you ain't getting out by yourself unless you're really talented.

When you use these effective options that are at your disposal, you can almost entirely avoid using your regular brakes on a steep downgrade. It is amazing how this works and it is also amazing how some clueless drivers will not take it to heart. You need to save your brakes for when you really need them.

As I am writing this today, the main story on the local news in Denver is of a driver that lost his brakes and drove right down an exit ramp crashing into an SUV, destroying both vehicles, and coming to a stop within several feet of gas pumps at a highway service station. Imagine the result had he hit those gas pumps.

The people involved are now in the hospital. Not knowing the exact circumstances of this wreck I can only surmise, that this truck driver was carelessly in a hurry, and instead of taking it slowly down this mountain grade, using a lower gear and the engine brake, he chose to use his brakes until they overheated and quit. He will pay the price for his ignorance. Bet on it. He is the responsible party.

If you are hauling a heavy load, it is best to take a little longer to get where you are going and avoid potential disaster.

Odds And Ends

4. DAC Reports & Protecting Your CDL

When you are starting out in the world of truck driving you shouldn't have any concern over a DAC report, but as soon as you do start out it will most likely follow you around. The DAC report is basically a history of what the trucking companies that you have worked for say about you. It is a very one sided deal and a bone of contention for many in the transportation industry. Depending on what is said about you, it can make the difference in whether or not you are deemed employable in the industry.

Basically a trucking company that you piss off can say whatever they like (or rather don't like) about you, and it becomes a part of your permanent record with DAC. It is like a credit report, in that you can contest information that you believe to be inaccurate. However, accuracy is of little relevance if they refuse to change it. They do not have to and the information most likely remains, but along with any explanation you may provide.

When you go to apply for a new position at your next company, most likely they will check your DAC report. A very high percentage of the companies in the transportation industry are affiliated with DAC services. If your report says that you had repeated accidents, violated company policies, and were fired for attempting to strangle your dispatcher with a length of garden hose due to his complete inability to get you even one decent load, that is what your next company will get to read about you. If you have enough negative information in your report, you may find it a bit complicated to get your next driving position.

The company can put fun little stuff in there, like whether or not you passed your drug tests or if you are eligible for rehire. The items that they report will remain on this record for years and can haunt you extensively if you have really messed up. This is one reason to be careful what you do with any particular company. Even if you quit and leave on friendly terms, they can say all kinds of bad things about you and get away with it.

Numerous stories are told about unhappy drivers abandoning their rigs at some exit out in the middle of nowhere. Under no circumstances should you ever do that. No matter how disgruntled of an employee you manage to become, I always suggest that you finish whatever job you are in the middle of and return your undestroyed vehicle to your home terminal.

It would not be right to do otherwise, even if you are dealing with completely unreasonable pea witted imbeciles at your company, there is never any reason to lower yourself to their level. So, never will you consider abandonment as an option. You are a professional and held to higher standards. While you are in fact obligated to entertain such thoughts, under no circumstances will you act upon them. They can't sue you for thinking of the most evil acts of destruction, but they can damn well come after you for the costs of going across the country to get their truck back.

Even though there is little to do about a damaging DAC report, other than to dispute it with your own explanation, there is something you can do to maintain a good record as a truck driver. If your company has put inaccurate things into your DAC report involving things such as accidents, but you can show them that you have absolutely no tickets or accidents on your Motor Vehicle Record, that is crucial. By all means protect your license.

Drive carefully at all times and especially in your personal vehicle. It is easy to get back into your car after two months on the road and do something erratic and stupid. If you are out of practice from driving a car, it can really be awkward. If you have become used to driving a huge tractor trailer all over the country, it can be a major adjustment to suddenly be at the wheel of something that takes off like a rocket.

The same is true after you have been away from your truck for awhile. It is easy to forget that it takes a little more time and patience than operating your car. Things happen more slowly in a truck and a short readjustment period may be required.

Whatever vehicle you are operating, do not speed excessively. Sooner or later you will get popped. Don't invite tickets. A clean CDL means more than a DAC report full of lies. DAC is there for one thing and that is to inform its members what your previous transportation companies want to say about you. You may have angered them by quitting and they want to get you back for it. This is really the best way for them to do it.

This is not to say that your DAC report is going to be nothing but vindictive lies. The truth is that much of the information is probably dead on accurate. Not everything on there is a detriment to your future as a driver. If your DAC report verifies much of what you include on a future job application, that is a major plus for you.

If you have always passed your drug screens, you have extensive experience in mountain driving, no accidents or company violations, and have stayed with your previous companies for an acceptable length of time, these are things that are viewed in a positive manner. Either way, it is to your benefit to have the most amount of information that makes you look to be a potentially solid fit as a new driver for their company. Companies are well aware that drivers and their previous employers often develop a serious adversarial relationship. It is nothing unusual in this field and it is not necessarily going to hold you back. Drivers usually have plenty of solid reasons for parting ways with their past company.

Whatever happens though, your official Motor Vehicle Record is your actual legal record of any trouble you may have gotten into on the road. No former company can put any information whatsoever on to that record. Keep it clean. On top of all of this, you want to remember that tickets with a CDL are more costly. As a professional, there is more expected out of you than just a run of the mill minivan driver. So do not ever forget to protect your CDL at all times. Got it?

<u>Odds And Ends</u>

5. The Big Blowout

Unless you are the ultimate king of good fortune, sooner or later you will come face to face with the inevitable misfortune of "the big blowout." That is to say that you will eventually be the potential assassin who is firing "gators" from the underside of your rig in an attempt to nail that minivan, that has been riding on your DOT bumper for the last fifty miles. You will most certainly get the eventual opportunity to deal with that phenomenon known as the exploding tire.

According to the Department of Transportation rules and regulations, you are permitted to use recapped tires on all but the two front (steer) tires. This means it is highly likely that the remaining eight tires on your truck and the eight tires on your trailer are outfitted with recaps. It is much cheaper for your company than using a new tire. Recapped basically means that an old used tire has been given new tread and a new life. Hallelujah!

In most cases recaps will work just fine, but as is apparent to anyone driving a few miles on the highway, many of these high quality tires have come apart and large portions of that nice tread (gators) are now decorating the Interstates of America. Such things are actually dangerous.

As I mentioned previously, I actually had one of those shiny new yellow VW Bugs riding endlessly on my bumper for many miles on a country highway in Colorado. This driver would not go past me even though he had numerous opportunities to do so. All of a sudden, there was a loud bang, and in my mirror I observed a large hunk of rubber shooting like a rocket from under my trailer and heading directly for the tailgater.

This obviously terrified driver swerved all over the road in an attempt to avoid a personal confrontation with my large tire piece. He was lucky. My shot was close but went a bit wide and to the right.

Seriously though, this driver is lucky that the front of his car wasn't wiped out. The windshield could have been broken and the driver too could have been nailed. This should be a lesson to anyone not to drive up closely in back of a big rig. If you have ever looked closely at a "gator," you will notice that it has nice sharp metal parts protruding out from the rubber. They are in fact very heavy and have the potential to kill someone if aimed properly. But, seriously again, these things can be a real threat to life. I would never want to be on a motorcycle and have to tangle with a flying "gator." There is little doubt who will win that battle,

There are quite a few logical reasons for the untimely demise of your rubber, but the most common explanation is inadequate tire pressure. This is probably accurate in most cases, but I have had several other causes also.

While these tire explosions aren't going to happen often, they will always happen at the most inconvenient moments, that is **when you are driving your truck**. How unusual.

One of my first blowouts happened on Interstate 15 about fifty miles or so east of Las Vegas. It was summertime and the temperature was well over 100 degrees making the highway into a veritable frying pan on which you could possibly torch a nice T-bone. It was hot! On top of that I had a near capacity load on the order of about forty-five thousand pounds in the trailer. A heavy load and a hot road is a good recipe for a tire to explode. There we go with the poetry again.

As for having the correct tire pressure in my trailer tires I do in fact confess to a certain laziness in that department as I believe do the vast majority of drivers out there. This is clearly visible in the huge number of "gators" littering the highways. I have a reasonable degree of certainty that such practice or lack thereof is more than the norm in the transportation industry.

While I always make my visual daily inspection of the tires, it is rare for me to actually get actively involved with a tire gauge and check for the accurate readings. If a tire looks low to me, I will inspect it more closely. It is amazing what you can sometimes find sticking out of your tires (important stuff like a couple of fingers off the driver of the minivan you crushed last week).

Many drivers go around their truck with a big stick (tire thumper) and bang on each of the tires to check for a flat. Although it is probably a good technique, I never do that. In spite of what anyone tells you, if a tire is flat or going flat you can see it has a problem by looking closely. If it is an inside trailer tire and I can't tell for sure, I might stick my foot in and give it a good kick. Inside tires are harder to tell because they may be held up and in place by the correctly inflated outside tire. It can be a little deceptive, but a tire that is going flat usually has a funny look to it. You can tell that there is something not quite right.

If a tire looks low, you can put air in it, but this is the real time to check it more closely. It is this low tire that may have a big nail it. It is just waiting for you to pull away from the safe confines of a repair facility at the truck stop. As soon as you return to the highway and get a few miles out into the middle of the desert, it will inevitably go kaboom. That is of course something similar to one of those Murphy's Laws of "if it can go wrong it will, and at the most inopportune moment." Uhhh, something like that.

Not all exploding tires make a big noise and some do. The one outside Las Vegas was inaudible to me. I was completely unaware of the death of one of my trailer tires until a driver pulled along side of me and pointed at the rear of my trailer. I stopped to look and there was the remaining carcass in all its exploded glory. At the other end of the spectrum and on the other side of the country, I was cruisin' down the highway in Virginia, when I swore I heard a cannon go off. It was a trailer tire which had chosen to take its own life at that moment. I was certain someone was firing off their cannon, until I saw that "gator" in flight. It was movin' right along.

At this point there are several things you can do and it often may be something that is a policy of your company. While you are not supposed to drive on the highway with an exploded tire such as I had, most drivers are going to do it anyway. You can advise your company and they can possibly authorize a repair truck to come to your location. This will cost them a piece of change for the on the road repair, but sometimes there is no choice.

Driving through Kansas one time on Interstate 70, I kept running into another driver who really wanted to show me that he had the faster truck. I was impressed. Being that my truck at the time was speed governed at 65, there was little doubt in my mind that he probably did have the quicker vehicle. Every time he came up behind me, he would zoom by and cut right in front of me. This was no big deal, but it was a minor irritation, and the fact that I wished upon him a torturous death of a thousand cuts is of little relevance here.

What did happen though made me laugh. He passed me one last time leaving me way behind. (It is often amazing how if you are on a road long enough, the same vehicles will pass you again and again. Maybe they are taking lots of breaks.) A short time later as I was approaching within about a mile of the weigh station, I noticed this very same truck on the side of the road. He had suffered from that inevitable confrontation with the exploding tire. Such a shame. I truly felt empathy for this buffoon. NOT! There were no exits before the weigh station and thus this fellow was stuck where he was and needed the tire dude to fix him up.

I won't say that you should never enter a weigh station with a blown tire, but the DOT officer can write you a summons for operating an unsafe vehicle on the highway, and then put you out of service until you get it repaired. I would not do it and clearly the guy with his fast truck was not going to do it either.

My situation outside of Las Vegas was a different matter. There were no weigh stations in front of me and my company (by use of the Qualcom) suggested that I make an effort to get to the repair facility in Las Vegas (that is the Flying J truck stop). I did and there was no problem in doing it.

Because you have so many tires on your tractor trailer (18 big ole tires), the fact that one of your trailer recaps has become non-functional is only of minor concern. It is most likely, that if you drive a little slower and be a bit careful, you will have no further complications on your ride to the repair facility. In most cases your company is going to want you to drive to the tire shop for repair and save them the excessive expense of an on the road fix.

Sometimes this is not an option. That fun experience with the yellow VW turned out to be a little inconvenient. Not long after my blowout, I got on to Interstate 70, looking for a repair shop. My company, of all things, suggested that I drive around the weigh station, that was just past the next exit and visit the then Rip Griffin (now a TA) truck stop repair facility in Limon, Colorado. As I have stated, I have little interest in driving around a weigh station for any reason, besides it is illegal to do so.

I did agree to give it a try. However, this was one of those very few times I have had the marvelous opportunity (**Not!**) to be hauling a load of hazardous materials. Against my better judgment and only in deference to the wishes of my company, I took that exit just before the weigh station. I only drove about a block before seeing the sign, that I dreaded. "Hazmat Loads Prohibited."

Had I not been encumbered with the hazmats, I most likely would have made an attempt to avoid the weigh station and get my tire fixed. But I will not risk whatever potential complications, that might have ensued by my driving through the town of Limon and getting busted by the ever present DOT cops. Here I am, not only with a blown tire, but also with colorful signs on all four sides of my trailer informing anyone that was interested, that I am driving through your town illegally with a trailer full of hazardous materials. It is not going to happen.

As I have said repeatedly, protect your CDL. Your company is not going to admit that it was they that told you to take your blown tire and your hazmat load around the weighing facility. You will receive the citation and you will be responsible for any complications in regard to your illegalities. It is not worth the potential problems that you might get yourself into.

I immediately turned the truck around and pulled into what is still a kind of mini Flying J (no repair facilities and few other amenities). As I informed my company, there I would wait for them to send me the tire dude from the Rip Griffin's up the road. They agreed and it was a done deal.

The company paid extra for the service, but I did not stupidly put my CDL at risk, as they would have wished.

Be assured, that your company is not worried about your potential to get a citation if they think it will cost them more money for an on the road repair. For the company it is all about profits. It is you and only you that are completely responsible for the protection of your driving record and the ability to keep your CDL out of trouble. Do not allow someone else to screw it up. You can do that quite easily on your own and without any assistance. Bet on it.

There is one other time that there is no way that you will be driving on to the tire shop for repair. This has only happened to me once and it unquestionably had the potential to become a life threatening situation. I was heading up Interstate 5 in Washington State one evening on my way to Seattle, when I got a real surprise. I was in the second lane over from the right side of the road and traveling at about 65 miles per hour.

Suddenly and with absolutely no warning the front right side of my truck sank down to where I was sure my front right fender was scraping along the concrete. I had a steer tire blowout. This is without a doubt, "the big blowout."

When this happens you had better not be playing with your cell phone, babbling nonsensical garbage over the CB, or trying to light your next cigarette. You had better have both hands firmly attached to your steering wheel, because this is one time that you are absolutely not in control of your destiny on the highway. All bets are off. You hang on tightly and get that sucker stopped fast.

There is a very real possibility that when this happens and you are not paying close attention to your driving responsibilities, that you can lose control and flip the whole tractor trailer over. If this was to come about it would most likely cause enough turmoil in your life, that if you survived, you would always refer to this as a "bad day."

When one of the steer tires (that is the 2 front tires) goes out, you can not steer the vehicle any longer with any kind of reliability. In my case, I was lucky. There was no one in the lane to the right of me. I carefully applied the brakes, managed to maneuver off to the side of the road, and amazingly stop in a perfectly straight line. It actually looked as if I had intentionally parked where I did. The fact is that this is just where I happened to get it stopped.

It is important not to panic in such situations and probably the only reason that I didn't was because I didn't have enough time to even think about it. These things happen without warning and very quickly indeed. This is the reason to always keep both hands on the steering wheel. You only need to have this happen once in order for you to kill or be killed. Never forget that you are in control of a lethal weapon and it can be very unforgiving. If you are fortunate, this will never happen to you.

Once I was off the Interstate (by maybe 3 or 4 inches), I climbed out the passenger side (no traffic, much safer) to observe the damage. To my surprise, my front right fender was undamaged and situated maybe an inch or so off the pavement. I was excited. Now all I needed was to hook up with the infamous tire dude of Seattle or some nearby vicinity. Herein lies the rub (Shakespearean stuff).

Now there may be truck stops somewhere around the Seattle area, but I never did find one. There were four other tractor trailers with which I was traveling to the particular event we were currently involved in. I had been ahead of all of them, but one by one they caught up and waved gleefully as they passed me by. One of them actually pulled over and stopped. He gave me the numbers of the nearest repair facilities and was again on his way to Seattle.

I expected this would take some time, but I didn't expect what I got. I called the numbers which were provided by the other driver. All I ever got from this was that happy little recorded response, "We're sorry, but the number you have dialed is no longer in service....."

Needless to say I was thrilled at my "sorry" response. After waiting an hour or so a Washington State Police officer pulled up behind me. He hung around for a minute or so. The last thing he said was, "I'm sure there are people around here that fix these things, but I don't know who they are." That was it and he was off down the road. Not his problem and not his concern. "Thanks so much, you xxxxing jerk!"

I spent the next hour or so trying to contact anyone. I finally got hold of one of my company representatives, who offered a credit card number to pay for the repairs. Unfortunately, she also had no idea how to contact the tire dude. I was out of luck. None of my truck stop guides mentioned a thing about any repair shop in the area and as it was now starting to get real late, I had to be thinking about a 24 hour repair facility.

At about this time another happy little Washington State Police Officer happened along. He stopped for a minute and was equally as helpful as the previous officer. Then he was on his way too. Obviously, important business to tend to down the road. To this officer I also say, "Thanks so much, you xxxxing jerk!"

After several hours of waiting for nothing and unable to obtain any assistance from anyone, I was rapidly departing from my comfort zone and retreating into an altered state of consciousness. I was genuinely pissed off.

I finally picked up the phone and called 911. "What's

Your Emergency?" I explained in as much detail as possible my dire situation. The 911 lady on the other end of the line explained to me in no uncertain terms, that my previous contact with the less than helpful police officers of Washington State should have been handled differently. She told me that they were required to assist me in the official procurement of the tire dude. Obviously, they were confused as to the accurate entailments of their job. Once again I repeat to those two helpful fellows, "Thanks so much you xxxxing jerks!"

Not to sound one sided and just for the record, I once had a blowout in my 1996 Corvette, on Interstate 15 in San Diego. A California Highway Patrol Officer stopped, and while I was complaining on the phone to the Corvette dealer in Colorado about the demise of my $300 tire, the CHP officer jacked up my car, pulled off the lug nuts, and actually changed that tire for me. I was absolutely amazed. He definitely had no obligation to do something like that and yet he did. That is something I remember fondly. I guess they just do things differently in California. What do you think?

Getting back to the 911 dispatcher in Washington State, she actually did get the official tire dude on the phone in a three way conversation. Not long after that the guy drove up with the correct size nice new (used) tire and shortly thereafter I was back on Interstate 5 and headed into Seattle. That was a long night, but fortunately it turned out right and I didn't flip the rig or anything. Absolutely amazing!

You never really know what will happen to your tires. One time I actually found a seven inch long railroad spike sticking out of one of my drive tires. Fortunately I was in close proximity to my home terminal and got it fixed fast. Your tires are of great importance as they are your one connection between your tractor trailer and the highway. Do not take them for granted. Check them frequently and it will pay off. Ignoring them can provide you with dire consequences.

<u>Odds And Ends</u>

6. Don't Let Them Cheat You, They Will Try

Just one more little addition to odds and ends is worthy of mention. When it does become time for you to move on to something else and leave your current company behind, they frequently have a sneaky way of saying good bye. It will come in the form of a minor money shortage with your final remittance. This can quickly develop into an adversarial relationship. As Don Knotts (Barney Fife) used to say, "Nip it! Nip it in the bud!"

On more than one occasion, I have been cheated out of a few dollars here and there, but only once did I fail to get it all. That was only because the more than thousand mile distance that I was from their terminal made it difficult and also not really logical to take them to small claims court.

This little rip off can come in various forms and is probably only worth going after as a matter of principle. I am a strong believer in principle. The principle for me being that if you try to rip me off, I will take you to court and if I'm right about it, I don't really care how small the amount. I want everything I have coming.

Not too far back, when I said bye bye to a company, I got a little surprise in my last pay check. They had charged me an extra $55 to clean my truck. When I returned to see about the specifics, it turns out there were none. There was no record whatsoever of my truck needing to be cleaned. I am willing to bet that they do this to each and every driver that leaves, but they will never admit it. I will also bet that not one driver has ever challenged them on it, until now. Surprise! Surprise!

When I leave a truck, it is pretty much in the same condition as when I received it. In this case, because I knew I was leaving I carefully cleaned out the truck. This cheap ass company was going to get everything they could. This is a company that would reuse their trip envelopes over and over again for years until they were raggedy, dog eared, and down right filthy. I anticipated that they would pull something and they did.

The trick here is to go right into the office and tell them you are owed money and let them know in no uncertain terms, that you will sue them in small claims court for that and several other items you are working on. You don't work there any longer and they are cheating you for their benefit. Be willing to take them to court and let them know you will not be taken advantage of, ever.

I had no problem getting a check for my $55, plus another little item I found later in which I had been shorted. If you are owed money, do not be intimidated. Speak up! You have nothing at all to lose and most likely you will not have to go to court to collect.

I have no qualms whatsoever about letting the president of a company know that if I do not receive full remittance in short order, that the county sheriff would be paying a visit into his office, where all the employees would see, and he would indeed be served with a notice to appear in court. Nobody wants to go to court if they don't have to and I guarantee you, that they do not want to suffer the embarrassment of being paid a visit from the county sheriff.

It is actually a bit humorous just to think about it. The process alone of actually having the head of your previous company served with court papers by the county sheriff evokes uncontrollable laughter. I think it is the thought of watching his face as the sheriff asks him if he is Mr. X and upon his positive acknowledgement, he is handed that nice little paper requiring him to come to court.

Nobody wants to go to court and it is generally not worth their time and effort anyway. If you are owed money by your previous company, you will most likely, upon your request and the advisement of the potential for their next meeting in a court of law, be paid what you have coming. In only two times that I have actually felt compelled to threaten to take someone to court for funds owed, I was paid in full. However, in the event that you are not paid, you need to be willing to follow through with your plan of attack.

Do not be intimidated and do not allow someone to rip you off. If you are owed money, say so!

Seeing The Sights

Seeing The Sights

1. The Best Reason To Drive A Big Truck

Aside from the obvious, that you are being paid to drive, the best reason for driving a tractor trailer is because you have the incredible opportunity to travel about the country observing everything that most people spend a fortune on for maybe only a week or two each year. It is in reality a non stop vacation and you are on it.

Instead of spending your existence in some god awful dull office, store, or warehouse, you are constantly out and viewing some of the most amazing scenery on the planet. And, on top of that, someone is paying you to do it. Is that ridiculous or what?

Not only that, but you are actually in charge. There is no one there telling you what you can or can't do. You are the boss. You may not own the truck and you may not be deciding where you are going and what you are delivering, but you are in fact cruising down the highway of life with the complete and unfettered ability to do damn well what you please and when you please. Be assured that you are responsible for getting to your assigned destination in a safe and timely manner, but how you do it is strictly up to you.

If you are going from Denver, Colorado, to Long Beach, California, and you have never seen Las Vegas, guess what? You have to go right through Las Vegas to get there. And, if you don't waste too much time playing video games at the truck stop in St George, you might even have time to check it out.

Personally, I like to stop at exit 33 on Interstate 15 in Las Vegas, park my rig at the TA truck stop, risk my life in traffic to get across the street, and go visit the Silverton Casino, which for me has one of the most incredible "all you can eat" buffets anywhere. This is an exception to the rule. This is a well run establishment with an incredibly delicious and wide variety of dynamite and inexpensive food. It is always worthwhile and highly recommended by me, except for the part about trying to get across the road.

Having been through Las Vegas countless times, this is my choice. Yours can be completely different. There are many ways for truckers to experience Las Vegas. You can park your truck at any of the numerous truck stops. There are shuttles, cabs, and all kinds of transportation to get you pretty much anywhere you want to go. As long as you manage your time properly, you are on your own. Have a marvelous time!

There are so many things to see as you travel throughout the United States. Literally every state has something to offer. Certainly some have much more than others to offer, but as you drive and observe, you will see many new things every day you are out on the road. There is a freedom about driving all over the country. You have time to think amazing thoughts as you roll about the land. You might even decide that you would like to move here one day. I always grab those little "Real Estate For Sale" books that you will see everywhere. It can give you a rough idea of what things cost in the area and if they might peak your interest.

If you pay attention it is astounding what you can observe. Not long ago, I ran head on into a tornado in the middle of Kansas. While not everyone would want this, I will say it was probably the most exhilarating moment I have ever had while driving.

I was on a two way, two lane highway out in the middle of nowhere when I observed this large funnel cloud drop right out of the sky. While it certainly raises your blood pressure a bit and may even rattle the nerves, I was never in any way in fear of my safety. I had the weather station on the radio, and the emergency voice came on and said, "Go immediately to your tornado shelter! Go immediately to your tornado shelter! Go immediately to your tornado shelter!" On and on it went. However, as I was already in my tornado shelter, there was nothing further for me to do.

I could not turn my 71 feet of tractor trailer around. So, I had the option of either pulling over on the side of the road, or I could keep going and hope to outrun it. No matter what I did, it just kept getting closer and closer. I began to think I was a tornado magnet.

I pulled over in back of a couple other local trucks, grabbed my camera, and hopped out onto the highway. The two drivers ran up to me and yelled in terror, "What do we do? What do we do?" Thinking quickly I held up my camera and said, "Here, take my picture in front of this thing." To my amazement these guys would not touch my happy little Nikon, and instead ran scurrilously down the highway to escape the oncoming peril and certain devastation.

Under the threat of being sucked up into the sky I chose

to fire off a few rounds of the Nikon. I actually took a picture of those two chicken drivers as they ran away. I got several good shots of the approach of the impending disaster before deciding to get back in the truck and move on down the road.

As I drove on, this damn thing just got closer and closer. I thought, "This is ridiculous. If I am going to be carried off into outer space, at least I will get a few more good shots to be preserved for posterity." Certainly someone will eventually find my camera and develop the classic final moments of my riveting existence.

As I kept going down the road the whirling doom was literally yards away from the side of my rig. Truly this was exciting. I should have been terrified, but I wasn't. I raised my camera, fervently anticipating a most remarkable photo opportunity. This will be tremendous. I aimed the lens with my right hand, while continuing to hang on tightly to the steering wheel with my left. At the precise moment that I was again ready to fire away, and just like clockwork, that damned miserable whirling monster instantly sucked itself back up into the sky to be heard from "Nevermore." It was gone and there I was left holding the camera in eager anticipation of capturing the next cover of "Big Storm Illustrated" magazine or some other such illustrious publication.

Fortunately I did get a few shots of the approaching nemesis for the record book. And yet, I'll never forget "the one that got away." Oh well, just another day in the life of a "professional tourist," errr uhhh storm chaser. The fact is I probably should have been equally concerned about the torrential rain and wind that followed immediately. I wasn't, and I kept on going until the storm was only a distant memory.

You may never run into such an event and yet you will have different stories to relate. Every day is different and what you see may or may not be memorable. Either way it will be more exciting than telling some obnoxious moron, that you are all out of fiber widgets until next week's shipment, or trying to explain to some irate customer that he did in fact make all those long distance calls to the phone sex girl and he would have to pay the $200 bill in order to maintain his phone service.

<u>Seeing the Sights</u>

2. Time Management to Get the Most Out of Your Driving Experience

In order to make the most of travel about the country, you need to plan ahead. You have to know where you want to go and how much time you will have to spend playing before blazing off to your delivery appointment. If you are going to be screwing around, you don't want to mess up and be late. You always want to be right on time for your pick up or delivery. Promptness is essential here and you want to develop and maintain a reputation for always being on time.

Sometimes you are given way too long to arrive at your destination. This might be because of a weekend or maybe even a holiday. This is where you will use those extra days to your advantage. It seems that pickups and deliveries are rarely made on weekends. It seems that the only folks that are working on a weekend are drivers and sometimes that can really suck big time. It can be annoying if you are just sitting around wasting time at some truck stop, but there are always better things to do.

This may require a little manipulation on your part, but when you are in charge of nearly everything you do, this should not be a problem. Be industrious and be creative. If there is something you really want to do you can probably arrange it. There are drivers that make a stop at all the local golf courses on their route to wherever they may be headed. If golf is a passion for you, why not get to play all over the country. You are a "professional tourist." Get out and experience the world. That is why you are here.

Let me give you a small example. I picked up a beer load

in Colorado on Wednesday, the day before Thanksgiving, and because of the holiday it wasn't scheduled for delivery in Southern California until the next Monday. Poor truck driver will have to sit around in his truck for an extra four days and miss out on the holiday. Not!

That's not to say you couldn't find something else to do for the holiday, but I blazed out to California, parked the rig safely (very important to park your loaded truck in a safe and secure area), and proceeded to spend the next four days hanging out with the family in San Diego. After having a very relaxing time with the folks, I jumped back in the truck and proceeded to make an on time delivery on Monday. As far as your company is concerned you were under a load the whole time. You worked right through the holiday and yet without using any of your actual accumulated time off, you just managed to pull off a short vacation.

I am not telling you to be sneaky and not let your company know what you are up to. They may actually be watching your every move on the Qualcom. However, the chances are good that they are paying no attention to what you or any other driver is doing. You can occasionally coordinate such events with your company. It is often a trade off that can be beneficial to both of you.

In my case, the company has the good fortune of obtaining the services of a stellar driver who is willing to keep on working through a major holiday. My benefit is the extra days off and paid trip to visit the family. So it actually can work out well for everybody.

The truth is that most company folks head home for the weekend and could not care less what the drivers are up to. If you think I am kidding, try and get hold of anyone at all in your company over a weekend. It is not easy. Just hope you don't break down somewhere on a Saturday night and expect someone to help you. Good luck!

Because you are out on your own, it is up to you how you spend your time. If you are headed for Sacramento from Omaha and you have an extra day in there, stop off in Reno. Park the rig. Go out and enjoy yourself. I like to park my truck at Sierra Sid's TA in Sparks (next to Reno). Although they try to make it complicated, you can walk around the back of the lot and visit the nice little casino located in back of the truck stop. Good food, tons of television sets all tuned in to different sporting events, and lots of gambling activities if you are interested. All those TV's lead one to the conclusion that the Steve Martin joke, "I go to church every Sunday, unless there is a game on," is undeniably accurate. There is always a game on somewhere.

Even if you don't have any plans it is usually most desirable to get where you are going in a timely manner. You never know what you will run in to. You need to watch the weather around the country and on the highway you are headed on. Avoiding that huge snowstorm a few hundred miles north of you by driving a little bit extra can be a relief beyond belief. Once you get where you are going, you can relax and then look for something to do. After all you just missed an extra foot of snow that might have held you up for days. And, thank your lucky stars, that you didn't have to deal with the evil chains.

Seeing the Sights

3. How Do You Know What To See?

In deciding what you really need to see while cruising between grocery warehouses, do not concern yourself. The point of being a "professional tourist" is that you should not start out with any preconceived notions. Every place you go has something to offer. Some places may take your breath away and about others you may say, "Never again am I going here."

The point of your overall driving experience is to take in as much of the scenery as possible. Check it all out. Sooner or later you will see places to which you are going to want to return. Maybe this is the place you always wanted to live and never knew it existed. Perhaps it is the place you always wanted to go and check out and now is your opportunity.

You will witness sunrises and sunsets that are absolutely incredible. And, since you are out in the middle of nowhere, you will be saying to yourself, "I am literally the only one out here seeing this." There may not be anyone around for a hundred miles and there you are witnessing something that is just stunning to see. You may see a cluster of shooting stars or meteors. When you are out away from any city lights, there are so many more stars visible in the sky it is just completely unreal to view. "Uhhh, I never knew that was The Big Dipper."

This is every day truck driver stuff. Many people will never have such an opportunity and yet you are actually being paid to see the sights. It isn't always what you are planning on seeing that matters. Every time you go to a new place, you never know what will be there. I was driving

157

north on highway 287 in very rural Colorado when I looked over and witnessed a huge eagle trying to drag what appeared to be a coyote carcass over a wire fence. I was astounded. I had only seen eagles at the zoo. He also has his picture on the back of your dollar bills and on various coins. I swear he stopped what he was doing and looked at me as if to say, "What are you looking at jerk?" He then proceeded to tend to the business at hand, so I drove on my way.

There are literally millions of things to see out there even if you have seen them many times before. If you are traveling east on I-70 through the mountains of Utah you will view those tremendously unique rock formations much differently than if you are in the exact same spot going on the west bound side. While sitting at a grocery warehouse and waiting interminably to get unloaded, may seem like the end of the world, I have never gotten tired of driving. I may get tired while driving, but I have never gotten tired OF driving, if that makes any sense. There is always something out there to look at. Just pay attention and enjoy the view.

The first time I was cruising west through Oregon on Interstate 84, I came over a hill and there it was, the incredible Columbia River. It is absolutely an awesome sight to see. In fact I was so enamored with the Columbia, that it was actually several trips later I realized, on the other side of the highway were some truly incredible waterfalls. I was so wrapped up in looking at that huge fast moving river, that I never once looked on the other side of the road.

Once was not enough. I had to travel that road several times in order to fully appreciate what was out there. Now the truth is that you can't always go everywhere with your tractor trailer that you can with your car, so you may want to plan on a return trip some other time in order to fully appreciate that of which you have gotten a taste.

Driving through all the big cities is equally exciting, especially late at night when the lights are on and the traffic is limited. You can actually enjoy some amazing skylines without fear of crushing any erratically driving pinheads in their minivans. Needless to say, I am less than fond of minivans and their usually less than competent operators.

I remember driving around in downtown Chicago in the middle of an afternoon rush hour with my tractor trailer. I was somewhere right near where they did the Oprah show. At one point I spotted the Sears Tower, which used to be the world's tallest building. As I nearly always carry my camera with me, I could not resist. I might never be here again. So in the middle of rush hour, I did in fact stop my rig on the middle of a busy street, turn on the flashers, jump out with my camera, and while hoping not to attract any small arms fire from irate commuters, I fired off a few quick rounds with the Nikon. Amazingly no one honked their horn, threw rocks, or even yelled obscenities. My endeavor was a complete success. I escaped with camera and film intact and several successful shots. Yes the nice people of Chicago were amenable to my photo op. Maybe they were thinking, "Damn tourist truck driver." Or, not. All I know is I got away with it.

It is for you to decide what to see. You know, "beauty is in the eye of the beholder." What you find to be of interest, someone else may not.

Up in Oregon, picking up a load of Douglas Firs for Christmas. Nothing like the smell of fresh pine trees.

Something a little different than a usual load and popular in San Diego, where customers waited anxiously.

Home Depot parking lot in San Diego. Not sure how I ever managed to navigate the truck into this spot, but the customers were thrilled to get these fresh trees.

Los Angeles radio stations always refer to truck accidents as "big rig over the side." Cruisin' down the I-5, this is definitely what happens when you don't pay attention. You definitely go "over the side."

Sometimes as a "Professional Tourist" you get to hang out with celebrities like the Tampa Bay Buccaneer's Mascot. An experience indeed.

Other times you get to pay homage to those you never had the opportunity to meet when they were alive.

Sometimes the scenery is breathtakingly magnificent.

Other times the scenery has the potential to suck you up into the sky.

The Best Driving Job of All

The Best Driving Job of All

1. What Is Really The Best Driving Job?

The best driving job is the one that you most enjoy doing. It is the one that allows you to spend the majority of time in your comfort zone and enjoying your life on the road to the fullest. This will most likely not occur with your first position as a company driver. It will take some time, lots of driving practice and highway miles under your belt, just getting to a point of being comfortable behind the wheel of this giant metal monster, and a bit of searching as the best jobs do not always jump right out and say, "Here I am." Additionally, the driving job that you find most appealing may be completely different from what someone else is looking for.

In stating my case, I will say that unless you are just thrilled by going from grocery warehouse to meat plant, to grocery warehouse to meat plant endlessly, I don't advise spending your life on the road. And yet if you are living a meaningless dull existence, not knowing what you really want to be doing with the rest of your life, there is literally no one that I would not recommend this too. Get the hell off the couch and go out and see the world.

Do not whine and complain that you "Can't find a job," "Uhhh they're just not hiring people my age," "Errr, I couldn't possibly drive that big thing." There are thousands of driving jobs out there and thousands of excuses for not seeking them out. These transportation companies are begging for drivers. Take advantage of the opportunity.

There are many different kinds of trucking jobs available. For me, I will limit my recommendations to what interests me the most. In my experience I tend to get bored easily and am not someone to stay with any company for an extended period. But, I regret only a few of the positions with which I have put in my countless driving hours.

I started out hauling reefer vans. These are refrigerated trailers, which while they are good to haul all types of freight, are most often utilized to haul things that must be kept either cold or warm. If you are hauling a load of potatoes through the Midwest at 10 degrees below zero in a snow storm, you are going to make sure your product doesn't freeze. You need to set your reefer (basically a generator that operates on the same diesel fuel as your truck) to keep the inside of your trailer above freezing.

Most of the time you will haul something you want to keep cold. It could be Coors Beer, some kind of fancy wine fresh from a vineyard in Washington state, ice cream, frozen Green Giant vegetables, or a load of fresh meat from one of those "eternally fresh smelling" meat packing facilities and slaughter houses.

The difference between a reefer trailer and a regular dry box trailer comes down to aggravation level. Occasionally they may pay you a penny or so more to haul reefers, but you will inevitably have to deal with, "What do I do now? The reefer shut down. I'm 200 miles from the nearest city. It is 102 degrees outside and my 44,000 pounds of fresh meat is starting to smell funny." With any luck you will never get to the funny smelling meat stage. If you do, you have waited too long for help.

A lot of drivers don't like to haul reefers as it is not worth the extra penny to put up with the potential nightmares. I did this for my first year on the road and trust me, I managed to see just about everything imaginable happen. You learn to deal with it and learn quickly where the nearest repair shop is for your refrigeration unit.

I once had a load of fresh meat (kept at 28 degrees it will not freeze the product) with five drops around the country. Almost as soon as I took the load, the miserable reefer shut off on me. After playing with it for a bit I realized there was a defective little switch that would not stay in the on position. I took a small piece of duct tape (Always carry a role of duct tape. It can be a lifesaver or just a load saver.) and maneuvered it into such a position that the reefer would remain functional as long as I did not run out of fuel. I kept that baby going for eight straight days, while making my deliveries.

I arrived for my fifth and final drop in San Diego at just before my 3 AM appointment. I was thoroughly pleased with myself at having kept that damn thing running for eight straight days. I walked up to the meat warehouse only to discover that "someone" had screwed up my appointment. This facility did not open until 8AM. At this point my reefer was very low on fuel, as in, it was on empty. Panic set in as I realized there were no truck stops in San Diego. My truck stop guide said there was one, but I have never been able to find it.

Of course the inevitable happened. The reefer ran out of fuel and after eight non stop days it finally shut off. I was not real happy at this point. I had no idea how long the remaining 5,000 pounds of fresh meat would remain fresh and at 3AM your options are really limited. What the hell could I do now?

When in doubt, beg. I walked back up to the meat warehouse and banged and banged frantically on the door. Finally someone answered. I explained my dire situation. They said that no one was there yet, but it would be ok for me to unload the product myself. "Hell yes," I would be glad to do it.

So after eight days of dealing with the evil reefer demon, I managed to get through it. Make no mistake about it. This is why many drivers will not deal with reefers. It is not fun and it is very easy to be removed from your comfort zone and thrown right into your panic zone. I actually spent nearly another year with a different company hauling reefers again. Why? I have no idea, other than that was what I knew most about, and fortunately they didn't do meat plants. How fortunate indeed for my keen sense of vile odors and carnal putrescence. Few things smell as bad as anywhere in the vicinity of a meat packing facility.

While I have both a tanker and doubles/triples endorsement I have never become involved with either. It is a personal choice to do so. Some drivers like it. I have absolutely no interest in them. There are so many different types of trailers and such (car haulers, bull haulers, flat beds, moving vans, etc.), that you really have to decide what you want to do and what is available for you to do. Many of these are specialty areas and you might not be able to start your trucking career with one. In other words, experience is required before you can jump in, and you don't necessarily want to anyway.

I prefer dry vans, but I have also on several occasions hauled flat bed trailers for a few extra pennies. I like knowing all the stuff I am hauling is going to remain in the trailer. I can't tell you how many over turned flat bed trailers I have seen where the product is scattered all over the highway. Maybe the product was not secured properly, or maybe the driver went around a corner too fast. I do not care. I want to know that when my stuff falls apart it will still be inside of the trailer I am hauling and someone else can pick it up at the delivery point. I do not want to look behind me and in terror watch as my trailer is spilling parts of the portable stage I just picked up all over the highway. No thank you. That is for another driver to deal with.

There is another type of trucking that for many is the best way to go. It is as an owner operator. You do not want to start out a driving career as an owner operator. Besides, the likelihood of your getting hired as an owner operator with no experience is probably very limited.

When you are getting started, you are going to make mistakes. You are going to have occasional problems. You may even bend the flanges on the sides of your brand new Freightliner. It is much easier to deal with that in somebody else's truck. Before you decide to get your own rig, you want to have experience behind you. Know in advance what you are getting into.

You can potentially make more (even a lot more) money by operating your own truck. You can also go broke in short order. There can be a lot to it. You have to decide if you want to get your own operating authority or operate under the authority of some company that you affiliate with. It can certainly get you more money. You have to decide if you want to lease a truck or just plain buy one. Oh, and when something breaks, **you pay** to get it fixed. I won't go into detail here other than to say, for me it is of no interest.

As I stated earlier, I am big on options. I like having the option to at any time say, "It's been real exciting, but I am out of here now. See ya."

When you own a truck and you decide you want to take some time off, you can. However, one thing that doesn't take time off are the payments required from your truck purchase. If you have a nice truck and you are making $400 payments each week, that does not stop just because you need a vacation.

If you think you may want to be an owner operator these are all things to keep in mind. While I confess to having thought about it, I am reasonably certain it is just not for me. I like driving, but without all the financial responsibilities that go with ownership. Before you make such a life altering decision, you had better be damn sure that this is what you are going to want to be doing for a long time to come. It requires genuine commitment. I am fully committed to maintaining my sanity. The ability to go out and enjoy driving and seeing all the sights, but with the ability to at any time end all ties to the transportation industry, is what matters most to me.

You can clearly observe that with so many aspects of trucking, that you have many choices as to which avenues you are going to travel. However, for me, the best one is explained next in detail. See if you agree.

The Best Driving Job of All

2. My Favorite Year, or So

As I have said, your best driving job is going to be a personal choice and what is right for me, may not work at all for you. My favorite truck driving job has virtually nothing to do with hauling freight around the U.S. There are absolutely no grocery warehouses, no meat plants, no loading docks, and definitely no mindless buffoons to wait on for ten hours to get twenty pallets loaded on to your trailer.

Chances are good that you can avoid most of those "not spotlessly clean and sanitized truck stop showering facilities." Even finding a parking space for your tractor and trailer is often not a complicated situation with my favorite. In fact, there may even be a very nice spot reserved just for you. Yes, stranger things have happened.

The potential for sleeping in a real and very comfortable bed nearly every night is not out of the question either. And it is in fact a very real possibility that you will have the opportunity to eat some seriously quality food on a regular basis. Of course all of these luxuries are paid for, and on top of that you also get paid. UNBELIEVABLE!! "Sounds like a hell of a deal. Can you elaborate further?"

What I am going to discuss here in detail is, for me, by far the most incredible excuse for a truck job that I can imagine. Possibly other drivers have come upon, what for them equates to a similar luxury, but I have yet to personally see anything that matches up. What I am talking about is touring.

Touring is not for everyone, because you can be on the

171

road for months at a time or longer. You will most likely have lots of time off, but it may not be within a thousand miles of where you call home. Then again it might. No guarantees.

You are probably going to need a year or two or even three before you can tap into one of these fun positions, but not necessarily. I was hired to drive for a tour involving the National Basketball Association and one of the other drivers had never even driven a big rig. This guy had absolutely no idea how to shift the gears and yet he got the job. I'm not sure how he even got his CDL, but this company was satisfied and it was none of my business.

There are actually tons of these jobs out there. You can see the trucks as they go down the highway. They often have very fancy and expensive graphic displays on the sides of the trailers or maybe on the front of the trucks. They are often absolute eye catchers. They may represent trade shows, concerts, or big events. You can see them everywhere.

Then again they may be in completely unmarked trailers for obvious reasons of security. Having said that, these positions are not always easy to find. Sometimes they are advertised on the major truck job web sites, that are prevalent on the Internet. Sometimes they are not to be found anywhere. You have to be observant in order to find them.

You can always ask a tour driver how to get in touch with his company. I have been asked often, "Hey, are these guys hiring drivers?" This is probably not the question to ask. If you value your job security, you might just say "No."

I actually got one touring position from a recommendation that had been given by someone with which I had previously worked. They passed my name around to several other people and someone finally called me. I had no idea how they even got my phone number and yet within 24 hours of the call, I was on a plane from Denver to Minneapolis for training and picking up the truck for the tour.

My first touring position came about by simply answering a job ad in the newspaper. While I had no previous touring experience, I represented something they were looking for. Ok, I confess that some, not all of these companies are looking for someone who can relate intelligently to their customers. Some freight hauling truck companies consider their customers to be the goofball pallet jack professional that is entrusted with loading and unloading bails of shredded paper from your trailer. This is not what I was doing or who I was dealing with on a regular basis.

The first tour I dealt with was for The Ford Motor Company and it involved their newest vehicle, the Mercury Monterey Minivan (Alright, mini- vans are ok, it's the drivers that are incapable of functioning in the real world and deserved to be hanged publicly). Many of the people I dealt with were executive types whose sole purpose in life at that time was to successfully market their new product.

I was given a shiny black Kenworth T-2000. It was by no means new, but it was unique. This truck had a brand new shiny black paint job that just glowed and it was impressive. I can't tell you how many times people said, "Hey that's a sharp looking truck. Is that new?" As I recall, this truck had six or maybe even seven hundred thousand miles on it, but with the new paint, which you could actually smell, it looked like it was right off the showroom floor.

This truck also had the distinction of being the only automatic transmission big truck, that I have ever driven. It was relatively awkward to drive without shifting, but I sort of got used to it after awhile. And of course, the fact that this sucker would hit eighty miles per hour on a flat road made up for most of the inadequacies. Once I got it rolling, I knew I could live with it.

It took me awhile to figure this truck out. The first time I pulled into a rest area with a trailer on the back, I could not figure out why the back of my trailer stuck out so far. All I wanted to do was have a quick nap, but no matter what I did it seemed to be too long. I finally got out my tape measure and discovered that instead of the seventy or seventy-one feet that a normal rig clocks in at, this baby was actually seventy-eight feet long.

The difference in this truck was partly due to the four instead of just two fuel tanks. It had two extra tanks to fuel the huge generator that I was on my way to Detroit to have installed. That was an experience. I started out from Denver pulling an empty flatbed trailer, that I was told was left over from a Bruce Springsteen concert. I dropped that off in Chicago and bobtailed (that is truck driving without a trailer) to Detroit.

Upon arrival in Detroit, I immediately checked into a very nice hotel, where I resided for several days. The next few days were spent welding my generator onto the back of the truck and then learning all my numerous functions on this tour.

This was my first time dealing with a hydraulically expandable show trailer. What an experience. These trailers are 53 footers and going down the road they look just like all the others. The exception being that they have some pretty fancy graphics on the sides and rear of the trailer. It also sits ridiculously low to the ground, because contained in the lower section of the trailer are some very expensive and fragile hydraulics (hundreds of wires and oil lines).

What makes these trailers unique is the little remote control unit contained in one of the belly boxes of the trailer. After a few adjustments in preparation, you plug the remote into the power, turn your generator on, and then watch the transformation. As you pushed various buttons on your remote, this trailer would magically change into an audio visual control room and a large meeting facility.

We would then set up steps and railings, such that people would be able to walk in and out of the meeting room (trailer). This was also climate controlled. Depending on where we were, the meeting room would be comfortably heated or air conditioned. Chairs and tables would be set up, along with several video screens. All this audio and visual stuff was controlled from a separate room so as not to disturb the ongoing meeting.

The purpose of this tour, which was sponsored by the Ford Motor Company was to certify their sales people around the country in regard to the new Mercury Monterey minivan and also the less expensive Ford equivalent (the name eludes me, but it might have been the Freestar, not sure). When set up the sales people would enter the facility, listen to a presentation, watch some videos, take a test, get free food, drinks, and consolation prizes, and they would be on their newly certified way.

It took a couple days of playing with the equipment to be sure you knew what to expect, and then you were on the touring highway. This particular tour had two teams, one for the eastern half and one for the western half of the country. My team did the east. My team included the audio visual technician, the tour manager, a very attractive young lady (who generally flew to each event and rented a car to get around) who gave the presentations, and one professional driver, me. Four of us altogether handled it all.

After several days of training and hanging out in Detroit at the Ford facilities, we were on our way. While the presenter flew around the country, the A/V guy and the tour manager drove to the event sights in a brand new Mercury Monterey. I hauled the rig. When we would arrive at each destination, I would strategically locate my rig exactly where we would be doing the presentation and we would either set up right away or head to the hotel and do it in the morning. Once we had it down, it usually took only about forty-five minutes or so to set the whole thing up. As a driver you get a bit of exercise, but I like that. It is so much better than any grocery warehouse and it was by no means complicated. It was in fact an enjoyable time.

As the sole professional driver, and after we were set up at each event, it was my job to hang out at the hotel and relax or really do anything I wanted. I could go and enjoy the sights or whatever, because I was in fact a "professional tourist." Amazing!!

After finishing up in a particular city, we might pack it all up and head right out, or there might be days off in between, in which case you either hung out at the hotel you were in, or headed to the next town and checked in early at that hotel. All these things were pre-arranged. Amazingly, you also had access to the hotel's complimentary computers in their business office and could usually get really accurate directions to each event. It was very relaxing and enjoyable to always be on vacation and to always know where you were headed to next. There was never any kind of rush to get there and you certainly weren't worried about mileage, because you were paid on a salaried basis.

Not every destination was a tourist town, but we did get to some nice places to be on vacation like Boston, New

York, Nashville, and Orlando, Florida to name a few. Additionally, there was also plenty of time to take in the scenery.

We started in Boston around the time of the Major League Baseball playoffs for the American League. Of course the Boston Red Sox were playing the New York Yankees. If you were in a restaurant in Boston, all you heard was how the Red Sox were going to kill the Yankees. Next we went to New York. When you were in a restaurant or bar there, it was of course no question, but that the Yankees were going to kill the Red Sox. Since we were so close, the tour manager and the audio visual guy actually hooked up with some friends and took in a couple of those games.

Because this was a tour and because you always wanted to look impressive, it was frequently necessary to search out the local truck wash. As much money as they spend on these tours, you want to always look good before getting to the event sight. In Detroit, I actually drove about a hundred miles out of the way to find a truck wash. Certain high level executives from the Ford Motor Company were present at the Detroit shows so we wanted to look especially impressive while there. And as I said these trailers are unique. This one cost about $750,000, so they certainly had a right to expect a professional looking operation and that is what they got.

While I never had to back into even one lousy loading dock, this tour with my seventy-eight feet of tractor trailer did require some serious maneuvering. One sight at a Ford facility in Atlanta, Georgia required that the tractor and trailer be located on the fourth floor of their parking garage. I still find it remarkable, that I actually managed to get it up there. This set up weighed in at 78,000 lbs, so that gave me a little concern over how solidly built this place was, but more important than that was just getting there at all. I had to back this thing up hill all the way, and around corners to get to the top of this facility. Fortunately the audio visual guy and the tour manager were there to let me know when I was close to knocking down any concrete walls.

The ability to get in and out of there was impressive and I was most definitely pleased with my performance. They got it right where they wanted it. This was not a place designed for a big truck and absolutely not one that clocks in at 78 feet in length. Fortunately we got in there at about three in the morning or we might not have been able to do it at all.

The Ford folks were pretty clear that they wanted these events held in exacting areas and you must keep the customer happy. At a Ford training facility in Florida, we couldn't get through the trees. The truck was too tall. So, once again, at about 3AM there were people climbing ladders and trees so they could cut off branches. All this just to get us to a very specific spot at their facility. They wanted it and they got it.

Only once did we have any mechanical problems and that was at the start up in Boston. We had a minor electrical malfunction. This would not be bad, but it had to be fixed. And, finding anything truck related in regard to repairs in the Boston or New York area was not going to be my idea of fun. How fortunate we were.

As it just so happened, the tour manager had a friend pop in for a few days to hang out with us on the tour. He turned out to be the former mechanic for the Miss Budweiser Hydro Plane. How fortunate and indeed timely. This guy knew exactly what we needed and in no time the problem was repaired. Finally, a no stress situation.

Anyway, that was my very first tour and I enjoyed the

hell out of it. That last event in Florida concluded it and I hauled my $750,000 trailer back up to Detroit.

As soon as I got to Detroit I was told they needed my services elsewhere. I parked my truck and locked it up. From there, a limousine picked me up and whisked me off to the Detroit airport. I took a plane from there down to Cincinnati, Ohio. From there I was taken over to the very luxurious Hyatt Regency Hotel in downtown Cincinnati. At this point I wasn't really sure what exactly I was there for, other than I was told I was going to pick up a truck and trailer and take it down to Miami.

I vacationed for several days in Cincinnati, checking out some of the local watering holes and such. The tour manager called me occasionally to tell me just to hang out for a bit. Yes indeed, I was suffering. NOT! There was a walkway from the hotel, that crossed over a main street to a local shopping area. From that walkway I could see the Cincinnati Bengal's Football Stadium and what appeared to be some sort of fancy trailer, but at the time I was not concerned.

Eventually they put my services to use. After several days of kickin' back and groovin' the tour manager took me over to the stadium where I was to drive what turned out to be that very same tractor trailer set up that I had seen from the walkway. It was the official Charmin Tissue bathroom trailer. It was in fact a one million dollar trailer, which was in reality a collection of fancy traveling portable restrooms. I never actually did see it completely set up except in pictures, but it required a whole large crew of folks to put it together.

Something had happened to the previous driver and they needed me to drive this unit down to the NASCAR event in Miami, Florida. After my very relaxing time in Cincinnati at the Hyatt Regency, I was ready to roll. I basically drove almost straight down to Miami. When I got there, I said good bye to ye olde travelin' restrooms and checked in at a nice hotel (I think it was a Marriot), where I had a suite of rooms. This was ridiculous. I had an extra bedroom, a kitchen, and a huge living room. This place even had multiple television sets. I mean seriously. Did I need all the extra room? Why not?

I hung out here for another day or so and then the tour manager chauffeured me to the Miami Airport, where I caught a flight back to Detroit. Once again the limousine picked me up and hauled me back to the shiny black T-2000, which was anxiously awaiting my return.

This pretty much put the wraps on my first tour. Keep in mind of course, that for all my fun and frolic, I was getting paid through all of this. There were no worries about sitting at some loading dock for eleven hours listening to ignorant excuses as to why they were not ready to load my trailer and no concerns over cents per mile.

When I actually did figure it out, there were days when I actually was getting paid dollars per mile, but since I was on a salary it was of no relevance. Either way though, I was paid. It did not matter if I was driving, setting up my show trailer, soaking in the hot tub or floating about in the hotel pool, working out in the exercise room, eating in some fancy restaurant at the company's expense, or just sitting around watching reruns on HBO.

I actually got to eat in some very nice restaurants, consume unusual quantities of adult beverages, regularly had access to very delicious catered foods, and one day I even walked out of the fancy hotel in New Jersey with something like twenty pounds of incredible gourmet cookies. If I didn't take them, they were to be disposed of and I couldn't allow that to happen. Knowing I could never eat all these before they became rotten, I chose to feed the local population of Canada Geese. I never realized how tame these things actually were or that they had a massive appetite for very delicious gourmet cookies. These things were probably sold for two bucks apiece and I couldn't get rid of them fast enough. I wonder if geese get afflicted with a sugar buzz.

I have absolutely no idea who actually paid for all my accoutrements, but I am certain that it was not the "professional tourist" driver. The driver was kept happy on this tour and had an altogether marvelous experience. This is the way to do it! "Professional Tourist" indeed! "Hell yes!!"

Mercury Monterey Tour - The Truck with 4 fuel tanks

Extra fuel tanks for the generator that was added later.

Truck & Hydraulically Expandable Trailer - expands out on both sides

T-2000 from the front and with both sides of the trailer expanded.

78 feet of Truck, Generator, and Trailer outside of Boston.

Trailer hydraulically expands into this large conference facility with video screens and room for many occupants.

**Audio Visual Room complete with a very happy A/V
technician at the controls inside the trailer.**

**Tour crew with the Author in front of a real Mercury
Monterey Minivan.**

The Best Driving Job of All

3. More Tours? Yeah! And It Gets Even Better

My next tour was probably my most favorite. This was an absolute kick in the ass. Kill me but I enjoyed the hell out of myself. This one started for me in Denver, where I picked up my next KW T-2000. It was a shiny yellow truck with a big ole orange on the front of the top of the cab. This tour was for the Florida Department of Citrus.

This nice truck had a super ten transmission, which basically means you don't always use the clutch and instead shift some of your gears by a flick of your finger. It takes a little getting used to and I prefer using the clutch on a normal ten speed, but this is not going to be a tranny class. You may never see one of these. However, this baby went 84 miles per hour (I won't admit how I know that, but this truck moved right along nicely), and I like that.

I bobtailed to a large non-descript warehouse outside St. Louis, where inside were housed some of the fanciest trailers I have ever seen. Obviously, I was not the only driver on tour. My trailer was nearly ready when I arrived. It was another hydraulically expandable unit. This one opened up to expose a stage, with video screens and had a big tube sticking out of the back, which actually part of an entertainment area for kids. One of the points of this tour was to get kids interested in drinking Florida Orange Juice (the real stuff and not from concentrate).

I then went up to Chicago to meet up with the other team members for the tour. I remember it was very cold. I came out of my hotel room after the first night there and the truck was so cold it had to be jump started. After hooking up with my other team members I parked the truck and trailer and we headed into downtown Chicago to stay at another nice hotel and get a bit of training on proper tour procedures and in dealing with the media (You must be prepared for the TV cameras and news crews). The next day I headed down the highway for Tampa, Florida. This is definitely the place to go in January.

My arrival at the Florida State Fair grounds went uneventfully. I contacted the guy in charge of the whole thing and he showed me where we would be setting up. It took a little careful maneuvering, but I managed to get the truck and trailer into our event spot right in the middle of a cluster of big trees (didn't bust a single branch). This is where the trailer would sit for the next three or four weeks. I then proceeded to disconnect from the trailer and head on over to the Hilton Garden Inn where I would be parking myself for the next three or four weeks.

Once we were all set up and ready to go, my entire responsibility on this tour was to make sure there was plenty of fuel in my generator to keep it going, such that all the tour video screens were functional and the electric power was on. Aside from that, as long as the generator was working, my time was my own.

There are numerous things to entertain you at the Florida State Fair. Because it is a state fair it is not just a bunch of carnival rides (They had plenty of those too). There were tons of animal exhibits, demonstrations, and shows. The variety was infinite. There was never a shortage of events to attend or things to do.

Yes, it is hard to relay my ecstatic enthusiasm for doing this as opposed to sitting at a meat packing plant for three days at a time, sucking in the "fresh" air of newly slaughtered and butchered cattle, and waiting for them to be loaded onto my trailer. Yes I can often hear the "moos" of those unhappy deceased bulls from the back of my refrigerated trailer. They were saying "please don't make me into cheese burgers." But seriously, doing the fair was so much more satisfying in every way, than dealing with the normal rigors of daily trucking life.

I got up in the morning when I wanted to and usually took the hotel shuttle over to the fair. If I had errands I could bobtail wherever I chose, but it was much easier to take the shuttle to the event site. Whenever I was ready they would come back and pick me up. All it took was a quick phone call.

There was so much to do at the fair, that I was pretty much over there every day checking it all out. On top of that, you always wanted to be there at four every afternoon. As an exhibitor at the fair, you were also entitled to a catered dinner every day. Some of it was downright delicious and it was of course free.

Many things were free. I also was afforded the option of attending concerts in one of the large pavilions at the fair. As an exhibitor, I got a pass that provided me access to free food and drinks before and during the show. There were all kinds of different events. I went to see the very classic rock of the band, 38 Special. It was a stellar performance and made even better with my access to the free food and adult beverages. "Yeah."

Apparently the various concert performers were also staying at the same hotel as I was, but I only observed a well known rap group, the name of which evades me at the moment. However I know I did see a famous rap group clamoring about the lobby of the Hilton Garden Inn.

This tour was also fun due to the involvement of local celebrities. Several of the Tampa Bay Buccaneers showed up at our event site to take photos and sign autographs. At those times there was a line in to our event a block long. The team mascot, actually a guy with a huge pirate head, was the big draw for the local kids. Although I had never seen him before, all the little munchkins were more than thrilled at his presence.

The highlight of local celebrities for me came in the form of several of the Tampa Bay Buccaneer Cheerleaders. They were a bunch of little cuties. They also posed for pictures and signed lots of autographs.

There was always something going on at the fair. We were positioned right next to the alligator show. This was fun for me, because in all the miles I have driven down south, I have only managed to see one lone gator sitting on a little island mound of dirt, and that was from quite a distance. All I heard about was how there are just alligators all over the place and yet I could never seem to see any. But here at the Florida State Fair, I actually got to see a "fer real gator wrassler" and some real alligators.

I was actually so involved watching events at the fair, that I missed Air Force One carrying the president flying right over the top of us. Right afterwards everyone was saying, "Did you see it?" I of course saw nothing. You really have to pay attention if you want to take in all the sights.

Only one time in the month I was there did we have a problem with that generator. A fan belt broke. What now? No video screens, no power, and no show for the Florida Department of Citrus. There would most likely be no repair shop anywhere within a hundred miles of the event.

It was then that it dawned on me that there was an equipment rental place, literally across the street from the fair, and with the same name as was on the side of the generator. This was almost the equivalent of winning a lottery. There was absolutely no chance that this was the same company, and yet it was.

We cruised quickly over to the shop across the street, grabbed the shop mechanic and said "You must come with us now." Fortunately he did and replaced the fan belt, and we were up and running again in no more than thirty minutes. Relief, when it could have been disaster, and yet, as I have stated previously, it always helps to pay attention to what is going on around you. You never know when it will pay off.

This tour ended much too soon for my liking, but nothing lasts for ever. On to the next ride.

Florida Department of Citrus Tour - The Truck

The Hydraulic Stage Trailer with tour vehicle in the background.

The Tour Truck side view

Citrus Tour Staff on the tour stage with the Author

Tampa Bay Buccaneer ex-kicker Martine Grammatica with the Author

The Best Driving Job of All

4. And More Touring

This next tour provided a bit more in the exercise department, but it was still a more than memorable experience. This is something that wouldn't come up often and yet I am sure that similar events are always ongoing. This tour was a commemoration of the 50th Anniversary of Sports Illustrated Magazine. This is not something that will happen every year, so they really did go all out.

This tour was already in progress when I joined it. In fact they also had a large event area at the Florida State Fair at the same time I was actively involved in orange juice. Although I actually visited their event in Florida, I had no idea at the time, that I would be joining them shortly.

This was a much larger production. There were actually five 53 foot trailers that traveled around the country for this one. Each trailer housed different aspects of the tour. My trailer held two very nice new Toyota show vehicles, several huge tents, thousands of free giveaway souvenirs (hats, shirts, Frisbees, etc.) and a very large and heavy display set up for Shaquille O'Neal's size 22 basketball shoes and jersey.

After all five of these trailers were set up at each event sight you were able to view numerous aspects of the 50th Anniversary of Sports Illustrated Magazine and several of the tour sponsors, like Toyota and Best Buy. Nearly everything involved in this tour was free for the public. There were free pictures of you standing in front of a special racing Toyota (trick computer photography), free prizes and souvenirs, and all sorts of promotional stuff.

One of the five trailers, which was brought in especially from Canada for this tour, was hydraulically expandable into a portable stage. It looked just like a big time outdoor concert stage. It had a light show and sound system with big speakers and such. There were several sound guys on the tour, who kept things going and even a regular DJ to run the events on the stage. It was all very professional and I believe they spared little expense.

There were probably twelve to fifteen people that traveled with this tour full time and several others, that would pop in with regularity to make sure everything was going smoothly. There were so many aspects involved in this tour that it was necessary to hire local help for its set up and operation.

Whenever we arrived at a specific event, there would usually be a large engine driven forklift already at the event sight to move some of the larger and heavier pieces into position. Several of the tour people would operate this. I never mentioned any previous forklift experience, as I had no interest in becoming an active participant in this department.

As this was a large endeavor, pre-planning was involved. Very often a large group of local Teamsters or just a group of laborers would be there to handle much of the physical stuff. But, being they were new to the event, it often required a bit of hands on physicality from the drivers. There were four regular drivers with this tour. The fifth trailer was either hauled by one of the four, or the company would actually hire someone to move it long distances. Each driver would help out with the major stuff and then we would each have our own set-up responsibilities.

I was entrusted with the infamous "Wall of Doom." This actually involved hooking together large metal poles with an allen wrench and then attaching to them large plastic banners which represented numerous past covers of Sports Illustrated Magazine. After doing this a few times, you get into a routine, and it actually comes together quickly. The "Wall of Doom" was so named because in a strong wind (of which there were plenty) the metal framing would occasionally come detached and fall apart. These things were seven or eight feet tall, so you really did not want to be hit in the head with a heavy piece of falling metal.

While I usually set most of this up on my own, occasionally the local laborers would assist. I preferred to do it myself, knowing that I might be found responsible in the event of an accident, even though some local guy might have actually been less than diligent in the assembly process. Fortunately, it never happened on my watch.

Set-up for this mammoth event with all of the extra local assistance generally took one full day, plus a few extra hours the next morning to wrap it up. Tear down took much less time. From the point that we concluded the set up, I would once again return to my full time duties as a "professional tourist."

For the event days, the drivers would take an occasional turn at hanging out at the event to make sure things operated smoothly. In reality though, there were so many people involved, all you ever had to do was enjoy the "sights." In every town, someone managed to hire lots of pretty young ladies and a few guys to hand out flyers and do incidental stuff to make the show run smoothly. It always did.

Because so many of the events were held in some very tourist oriented places, you were generally surrounded by things to do. You could either hang around at our event or go out and enjoy the sights. I did both.

The hotels we stayed in were absurd. I could not believe

that one minute I am out driving around in a big truck and a few minutes hence, I am relaxing in what is known as the "heavenly bed" on the forty-third floor of the Westin Hotel in downtown Seattle and overlooking the boats docked at the local harbor. Aside from being up in the Empire State Building, I have never been so high off the ground. It was spectacular. It did take awhile for the elevator to get to you when you were up so high, but it was worth it for the incredible view.

While we were in Seattle we were set up right next to the famous "Space Needle" from the 1962 World's Fair. This is right in the middle of downtown and where it was all going on. With lots of time on my hands, I needed to figure out what to do.

Something I always wanted to do was meet Bruce Lee. It never happened and yet since he was resting peacefully in a Seattle cemetery, I thought I might pay him a visit. I asked the concierge at the Westin how I might get there, and while I could actually see the corner of the cemetery from my room, he said it is way too far to walk.

All I thought was that, if you really want to go visit Bruce Lee, you had better be prepared to handle a bit of exercise and without complaint. So, I grabbed my little Nikon and headed out. It was three miles of serious up hill walking and worth every block. Any self respecting "professional tourist" should certainly be prepared for an occasional workout.

I got there in no time and managed to grab another visitor in order to capture a couple camera shots of me standing next to Bruce and his son Brandon, who also resides there. Three miles up and three miles back and worth every minute of it. Yes indeed, another truly memorable experience as a "professional tourist." When I got back I looked into visiting

Jimi Hendrix. He was seventeen miles from the hotel, to which I said, "uhhh, never mind." I have my limits on walking and seventeen miles is just a little beyond. I was already getting plenty of exercise in setting up for this tour.

When looking for other things to do, it is actually a kick to just walk around and see the local sights in various towns and cities. As a guitar player, I always enjoyed checking out the local Guitar Center stores. You could actually go in there and keep up your practice on the wide variety of very nice instruments that were available for your perusal.

Sometimes when you are staying at a very fancy hotel, trying to find sustenance without the very fancy prices presents a minor challenge. Usually though, if they don't have plenty of food at the event sight, you can nearly always find the local fast food chains nearby. From my hotel room on the forty-third floor in Seattle I could actually look down and to my astonishment, there was in fact a minuscule golden arches directly across the street. "Ah yes, that was all I needed."

It is amazing how when you stay in a nice hotel, there are often useful amenities such as a business office. You might have free Internet access, (useful to print out maps to the next event sight or even all of the event sights), copy and fax machines, etc. If you really became enthusiastic, you could easily spend everything you made buying gold coins on Ebay. That really is too much free time on your hands.

Very often free breakfasts were supplied and some of them were really substantial. You also can use your various hotel reward cards to get more free stuff, room upgrades, or whatever you want. There are always bonuses to be explored. Ahh the life of a "professional tourist."

Some of the other Sports Illustrated Events took place in Southern California. From my hotel rooms I had several different views of the Pacific Ocean. I remember watching the news on TV from my room in Long Beach, California, as they were discussing the world's largest tanker that hauls thousands of cargo trailers around the world. I looked out my window and there it was right in front of me. Unbelievable!

I also had a partial but interesting view of the Queen Elizabeth ll cruise ship which is docked there now on a permanent basis. Seeing such sights is tremendous, especially knowing that people regularly pay big money to do what you are being paid for now. You are always on vacation.

One of our events was set up right at the Santa Monica Pier. We were literally inches from the sand on the beach. Being right next to the pier we had plenty to do there also, after setting up. The ocean breeze was incredible and highly conducive to a work atmosphere. When you stop at a place like this for a week or so, you just don't want to leave.

It is always strange when you are driving a big tractor and trailer into an event and you frequently see those signs with a picture of a truck and an arrow going through it. We went many places where you were not supposed to drive a truck. The reasons were sometimes obvious. "You can not get a truck down this driveway and around this corner. It is not possible." However we always got where we were going without fail. Sometimes it took a little extra effort, but especially since we were expected, it all worked out.

We spent a couple weeks in downtown Chicago running right through the Fourth of July. This was also spectacular. We had to set it all up right next to the Navy Pier, which is a huge tourist attraction in Chicago. I arrived earlier than the rest of the "professional tourists." I checked my truck and trailer into the Chicago Marshalling Yard, which is like a big pay for parking lot for big rigs. The attendant almost forgot to charge me. When the guy saw the fancy graphics from Sports Illustrated on the side of the trailer, all he could think of was that he really wanted a hat. I wish I could have gotten him one, but they were absolutely buried at the front of the trailer. The fact is that when I left the facility a few days later, I'm pretty sure he did forget to charge me for an extra day of storage. He still wanted a hat, but I still couldn't get to them.

After parking the rig, I took a cab over to the W Hotel, which is kind of a fancy modern and expensive hotel. When you check in, the lobby is dark and filled with exotic looking candle light. It is downright strange for someone who has just driven halfway across the U.S. in a big truck to all of a sudden be in some kind of luxury facility where much of the clientele is adorned with ties and jackets or evening gowns.

It cracks me up because here I am checking into a fancy hotel in my raggedy old jeans and a T shirt and probably reeking of diesel fumes from the spilled fuel I managed to walk through at the last truck stop. Then you check into this luxurious room which is way up high and overlooking Lake Michigan and the Navy Pier. It is stunning to say the least. Here you are, trucker dude, looking out a window at an incredible view and surrounded by some absolutely stunning architectural masterpieces. This is not what trucking is supposed to be about and yet it can be.

Since our event ran all through the Fourth of July, we also got several chances to view extensive firework displays, and right from your hotel room if you didn't want to battle with the crowds of people. I had plenty of time to travel all around downtown Chicago and see all kinds of fun things. Once again, this is stuff that some folks will pay big money to do.

The final stop on this tour was in New York City. "Oh no! Not NYC again! Terror!" Actually as I stated earlier, this is one of the rare times, that I was on a cell phone while driving. I had to get directions to Shea Stadium and the Arthur Ashe Tennis Stadium and I was actually sitting in a massive traffic jam getting ready to cross the George Washington Bridge. This is a thrill not to be missed, even if you only do it once.

The event sight for this show was directly in front of the entrance to the Arthur Ashe Tennis Stadium, where they were starting to get ready for the U.S. Open Tennis Tournament. Much like past events, it was a challenge to get all five trucks and trailers into the event and properly spaced. It was on a par with circling the wagon train in the old westerns, except these bigass trucks require a hell of a lot more space. However, as always we succeeded and managed to get it all put together correctly.

Our hotel was a very nice Sheraton, located somewhere around Chinatown. I'm not really sure where, as we were being chauffeured around in one of the tour vehicles. I have no idea how these people would find their way around in NYC, but they did.

Of all the places we went where the wind blew, you would never have expected to have a problem in New York City. This was the one place, that a couple hours after set-up I got a call saying that one of the tents had been blown apart and the frame bent beyond repair. I was also one of the only tour folks to answer my phone. Nearly everyone else was in dispose or possibly had retreated to the bottom of the jug by that time. Fortunately we had replacement pieces and the repairs were completed within a couple hours.

On the last night of the tour, I recall sitting in a karaoke bar next to the hotel with most of the tour folks. This would not be particularly odd except for the fact that we were in Chinatown and instead of the words to the songs being in English, the lyrics to each song were flashed across a big screen TV in Chinese characters. It was hysterical. The bartender knew all the tunes and was singing along to all of them. However, she was doing it in Chinese.

This final tour night was equally memorable in that, someone from the company walked into the bar and said, "Hey, the drinks are on the company." That is just about the last thing I remember with any clarity about that night. All I had to do was walk about thirty steps back to the hotel and take the elevator up to my room. It worked.

This company really did take good care of us. They even supplied us with our own Nextel phones so we could stay in touch. They had walkie talkies in them which were amazing. We could make calls whenever we liked without restriction. After the tour ended we got to keep our phones and they continued to operate for the next couple months, free of charge. I like free stuff. Have I said that before?

With the tour completed, we had to escape from New York into New Jersey where we would unload all the trailers. On that next morning after the night before, my phone rang. It was one of the other drivers calling to say we only had minutes to get our trucks and trailers out of the area, because the New York City Police were shutting everything down for a baseball game at Shea Stadium and placing large barriers across all the roads that were our potential escape routes.

Try as I might. There was no way, that I could have gotten over to the stadium and out of the area in the next hour, but I did make an effort. I managed to get hold of a taxi cab and when I finally got to my rig and got it started, I could easily see that the barriers were already in place. I was sure I would be sitting all day because of this, but I gave it a shot anyway. Surprise! Surprise! Surprise! Maybe it was the shiny Sports Illustrated fancy graphic display on the sides of the trailer, but as I approached the barriers, those nice folks of the NYPD got out of their cars and pulled those big ole barriers away just for me to get through. I was excited indeed and once again we were back on the highway.

After a couple more days hanging out at the hotel in New Jersey, we got everything unloaded and we were on our separate ways. The first thing I had to do was to take the portable stage trailer back where it came from, in Canada. I wasn't altogether excited about the prospects of driving into a foreign country with a big truck.

There are always things that can go wrong in another country even if it is only Canada. The laws are different and I for one am not familiar with them. There is certain paperwork that must be tended to at the border crossing and it does take extra time. Some drivers do this every day and so it really isn't that big of a deal. I do not.

I probably sat around for an hour or so before I got an official approval to cross. It was all very uneventful until I got into Canada. Leave it to me to find a crossing where all the road signs are in French. I have no idea what any of the signs said, including the one which probably said "Weigh Station Ahead." This is the only time I have ever driven past an open weigh station. I didn't even notice it until I had already driven by. Amazingly no one came after me, so I really have no idea what they expected me to do. It was a harrowing experience, but I survived it.

I will say that kilometers go by a whole lot faster than miles. I arrived at my destination in short order. I dropped off the stage trailer and was on my way back to the United

States. Back at the border crossing, the U.S. Customs Agent was curious as to why I wasn't hauling anything, but my Sports Illustrated stage trailer explanation was good enough and I was on my way in about ten seconds. This was a bit quicker on the return than it was to leave. Thus an end to another fun-filled journey as a "professional tourist."

<u>Sports Illustrated 50th Anniversary Tour</u> - The Truck
and the Author

<u>SI TOUR</u> set up at the beach next to Santa Monica Pier
in California.

Ah yes, Nothin' like hangin' out at the beach in Santa Monica. The rough life of a "Professional Tourist."

As you can tell, this tour required extensive set up, but where else would you rather go to work? Seriously!

The SI Truck with the Portable Stage Trailer up north in Canada.

Some of the traveling S I Tour Crew & Drivers with the Author relaxing after setting up in Chicago.

The Author and a small part of the "Wall of Doom" in Pasadena across from the Rose Bowl Stadium.

The Author with a closed up Portable Stage Trailer.

The Best Driving Job of All

5. Even More Touring and the World's Scariest Road To Drive a Truck

Just because you are on the road for months on end doesn't mean you will never get to see your family, but it can be a challenge. One of the other drivers from the Sports Illustrated tour was on the road for over a year straight and yet he had a wife and four kids waiting for him back in Arkansas. I don't think I could have done that, but he managed. This has got to put a strain on a relationship. He did try to make amends by flying his wife into New York City for the end of the tour. He took her to see shows on Broadway and some of the other sights. In spite of it all, he was heard to say that he would be giving up life on the road in favor of driving around on a forklift in a warehouse in Arkansas. You never know.

Even during some of these tours I have managed to visit friends and family. I have been in the middle of a tour and had some spare time. You learn to make use of it. I can't say this would happen for everyone, but I have in the past, incredibly been given a free reign to do as I please with my time off.

I not only was paid my salary, but got extra pay per mile for doing things outside the tour. While in the middle of one tour, I picked up a portable stage on a flatbed trailer, that was to be used for a single Dave Matthews Band concert in Golden Gate Park in San Francisco.

After dropping off the trailer in San Francisco I bobtailed down to San Diego to visit my family for a week. And you bet, I was paid for the whole thing. Let's see, uhhh, is that as desirable as sitting around at various grocery warehouses waiting for the big load or unload? You have to decide what will work for you.

The last tour I will talk about is one which started for me in New York. I was scheduled to pick up one of the trailers for the tour at a place called Floyd Bennett Field. It was New York City's first municipal airport and was opened in 1931, but doesn't get much use any more. This air field is in the southeast end of Brooklyn and to the best of my knowledge, the only way to get there from where I was, was to travel almost the entire length of Flatbush Avenue.

The chances are that anyone that tells you they drove all the way down Flatbush Avenue in a big rig is either lying or they have to be crazy. I will confess to the latter. What is required in order for one to actually traverse that twelve or fifteen miles is beyond the comprehension of a normal truck driving fool. I can't even remember exactly how many miles I went on that road due to the thousand different distractions that occurred. What's worse than that is that I had to go back the same way. In other words, I did Flatbush Avenue two times in the same day and I am here to tell about it.

It is almost indescribable to try and say all that I viewed. This is a road through the center of Brooklyn, that must have had a million people going in all directions at once. There are two normal travel lanes going in each direction (as in 4 total driving lanes). There is also a parking lane on each side of the road. In reality there is not a spot on this road not covered either by people in cars, buses, on bikes, in wheel chairs, pushing baby carriages, walking, running, and even passed out on the side of the road. You literally cannot see the pavement for all the people and vehicles.

Put a big truck into this mix and you can expect chaos. The thing about people in NYC is that everybody is going in a different direction and nobody is willing to stop. Forget the parking lane. There is no parking space there, so everybody either double parks or triple parks. This means that both your travel lanes are blocked by people parking their cars. In order for you to get by you must drive across the highway into the oncoming traffic.

When a police officer is pulling someone over, it is not to the side of the road. It is right in the middle of the road. Once again you must maneuver out into the oncoming traffic in order to get by. It is complete and total insanity. People on bikes are constantly riding right in front of your truck and then disappearing under your hood. You never see them again and you wonder if they are under your front wheels as you roll slowly on down the road.

There are ambulances and fire engines literally on every other side street tending to who knows whatever acts of inhumanity that have been perpetuated. Sirens are going off everywhere. Some of the strangest looking folks you can imagine are wandering about. Actually there is nothing unusual about these sights. This is typical of New York and yet there is one key here. It is that you should NEVER EVER have to operate a big truck on Flatbush Avenue in Brooklyn. EVER! It is horrible. It is the ultimate chaotic experience.

The fact that I did this during rush hour may have been the partial culprit, or so I thought. But I also drove into this without a trailer on the back of the truck. I bobtailed in. I finally arrived at Floyd Bennett Field just as the sun was going down and had to wait several hours while they packed up my trailer completely. At least I will be going back at night after things have quieted down and my heart rate has had time to return to the near normal range.

I finally got out of there somewhere around eleven that

night and proceeded back into the jungle from whence I had come. This time I had a 53 foot trailer attached to the back, but by now everyone should be home in bed. Right? Of course.

Of course NOT! I swear there were twice as many people on the streets at eleven as there were during the afternoon rush hour. It was absolutely unreal. What a zoo! But as I was cruising carefully down this maze of potential disasters, it suddenly occurred to me, that if I can successfully navigate Flatbush Avenue in a big rig, there is not a place on the planet, that I can't drive.

Once again I was traversing the ultimate chaos. As I gradually approached what I knew was my turnoff point, my confidence level was absolutely soaring. I was the baddest of the bad right now and you better stay the hell out of my way. Just as I reached my peak of confidence, I also arrived at the one and only road I knew would take me back across several bridges and out of New York City. It was at this point my mind returned to reality, when I saw the sign that said, "NO LEFT TURN."

In only two seconds my whole outlook on life had changed. Where was I supposed to go, if not down this damn lousy road? I was already exhausted from my previous journey in the opposite direction and was not going to get lost in the middle of the night in NYC. Sometimes a snap decision is required. I did what any self respecting driver would do. I TURNED LEFT! Screw it! This is the way I was going to go. Amazingly I looked everywhere in anticipation of those flashing lights of the NYPD. There were none. I had made it successfully. Nothing else could possibly go wrong. I was going to make it out.

I think I maybe got two blocks before I saw the flashing lights on the big sign up ahead that said, "Bridge Closes At

Midnight For 8 Hours." I think I had maybe 3 or 4 minutes to get about five miles or so to the bridge. I looked at my watch and said, "I am going to get across the bridge and I am not going to sit here all night." I drove that happenin' red KW T-2000 like it had never been driven before. (Oh yes, I was now driving a red T-2000. They all looked alike, but had new and different paint jobs for different tours) Talk about a speed shifter bangin' the gears. I was flying. Finally, I could see that damned bridge ahead. There was some sort of motion going on, but I was too far away to tell what it was.

There were no other vehicles on the road. I could now see in front of me, that they were starting to move the big concrete barriers. I had to make it, so onward I charged. Closer and closer I got and then, I was through. Holy crap what a night! Just as I passed through they pulled those barriers across the road behind me. No one else was going through tonight. Hell, I probably had two or three seconds to spare. No problem at all.

The relief overwhelmed me and I drove on for several hundred more miles before stopping somewhere in the middle of Ohio. After the New York experience I always tend to keep driving until I know I am completely out of there. In this case central Ohio would work fine.

Oh uhhh this next tour? This was for the TV show, "Meet This Old House." It was a tour of Home Depots, and most of the time I was the only driver. It involved two fifty three foot trailers. I would take one of the trailers into a town, park it at some local storage facility and go back and get the other one. Sometimes there were weeks off between the shows. I think it had something to do with the guys from the TV show filming their series in between the tour dates.

All of the five guys from "This Old House" were

supposed to trade off, but most of the time it was Kevin O'Connor and Tom Silva that were hosting it. They would answer show questions, promote stuff, give away prizes, and do pictures and sign autographs.

Either way I had tons of time to do other stuff. It was actually some time during this tour, that I did the stage thing for the Dave Matthews concert and then took a week off to visit my family. I always had plenty of time to get both of my show trailers there, and I was always getting paid no matter what I was up to.

When I think about touring, I know that because I have an absurd ability to drive way too many more miles than I am supposed to, that I can actually make a bit more money hauling freight than I can by being on tour.

Who cares? It is not only about the money you can make. It is about enjoying your very short existence. I would not trade the fun I had on those tours for any other type of trucking job. Unquestionably, they have been the best driving jobs of all.

Meet This Old House Tour - Tour set up with cardboard action figures included.

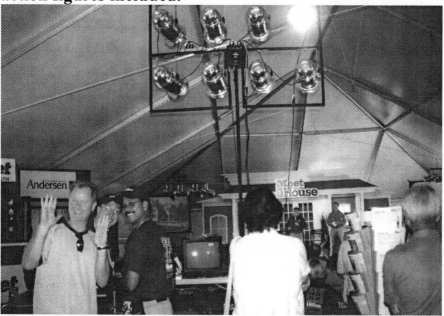

"Old House Tour"- the Author, Tour Staff, & Tour Stars way in the background.

Tour stars Kevin O'Connor & Tom Silva speaking to the audience in Los Angeles.

The Author with "Meet This Old House" star Kevin O'Connor.

Make Up Your Mind and Jump

Now that you've had all the possibilities explained to you, you can make up your mind. There is nothing at all complicated about driving a truck and there is nothing complicated about making up your mind to jump into it.

I had no problem getting into this, because I have never had even a remote intention of making this my life's ambition. I have never had any preconceived notion whatsoever, that I would be doing this for any more than a year or two. The fact that I have put in more than that means just one thing. I must be enjoying this to some degree. Very few people will ever admit that they always wanted to be a truck driver. I think I actually heard one guy say so, and he was about as bright as a small appliance bulb.

You do not have to be an unemployable mutant buffoon to go out and drive a big rig, nor do you have to be a brain surgeon. While this may be a question of major debate, not all truck drivers are complete imbeciles. Although, they are often treated as such by numerous shippers, receivers, and even the Mensa employees of the company for which they work.

For me there are two main reasons for doing this. I am getting paid and I am getting to see so many thousands of incredible sights for which most people pay big money for the privilege. It is mind boggling to me that more people don't check it out. The opportunities to see just about everything around the country are limitless. If you see something that really excites you, you can take a happy little family vacation and go back and visit. But if you never give it a shot, you may never know what's out there to see and experience.

There are actually places, that since the events of September 11, 2001, you are no longer allowed to go with a big truck. I had the incredible opportunity to cruise through Hoover Dam in Nevada. Due to obvious security reasons, this is no longer allowed. Take advantage of what is still available to see now, before they cut that off too. Nothing surprises me any longer.

This is such a great opportunity if you are single to get out and see what is around you. If you have been married for many years and your kids are all grown and out the door, chances are your spouse would love to see you out on the road and may on occasion even like to ride along. Retired and looking for something to do? Why not collect a pay check and get to travel. If you are married and have nothing tying you down, maybe you want to learn to become team drivers. Who knows? Once you get this all down, it is almost as simple as driving a car. Just watch those mirrors.

If you have read this book, there really isn't anything else you need to know. It is all here and if it is not, it ain't important. Trust me on that. If you are not going to be able to do this, you know by now. If there are things that are holding you back deal with it. If you have a young family and can't hit the road, then maybe some other time will be right for you. It's never too late to get started and the opportunity may always be there. You never know.

As I've said before, I don't think I would be willing to do this if I had a wife and family sitting at home. It is just too easy for people that are separated for extended periods to start living different lives. You can easily start to grow apart. For someone in this situation, maybe a local driving job would work. However, in my experience, local driving jobs are boring. That in fact is not the purpose of this book. Anyone can drive a truck around the town in which you are living. That is like driving in an endless rush hour all day or night. I have tried it and it is not for me. Forget about it.

Now if you are a big time, high level executive, and making more money than you know what to do with, you can already afford luxurious travel accommodations. I do not recommend this for you unless you are just plain sick and disgusted with the corporate world and just want to get away from it all. It could happen. Couldn't it? This stuff is not for everyone. Yet I think for many folks, it is worth it to devote a couple years of your valuable time to a new life full of adventure. You can always walk away from it. Can't you? You bet.

Oh, and if you are actually looking for one of those fun filled touring positions, there are really any number of ways of tracking them down. Once in a while you might see one listed in the help wanted section of the local newspaper, but not very often. That is in fact how I came up with my first touring position. So, it can happen that way.

Several well known touring companies are listed along with the rest of the truck jobs right in the middle of some of the truck job web sites. All you have to do is look them up. Just put "truck job" into your happy little Google search engine and it will all appear magically before you. I promise you they ARE hiding right there amongst the freight hauling companies. I'm not giving out any names, but they are very much in attendance with all the others. Do your homework and it will pay off.

If you do decide to drive a big truck, these very same fancy tour trucks get fuel at the same place you will. If you are genuinely interested, do not hesitate to walk up and ask the driver how to get in touch with his company. Do not ask that brilliant question, "Hey man, are you guys hirin' drivers?" That is most likely not going to elicit a positive response. That's like saying, "Hey, I want your job dude." The answer to that will probably be, "No, I don't think they are hiring." With that you will have accomplished little.

All you want is the contact information. You will then get in touch with the company yourself and find out just what it does take to become one of their drivers. A driver may be willing to divulge to you all sorts of invaluable tidbits in regard to how you too may get happily involved. Then again he may not. If you come across well, you never know what you can discover. Either way, the driver will most likely not get you the job. Get the contact information and sell yourself to the company.

There are other ways to track these companies down. Some of these fancy show vehicles may even have contact information posted amongst the fancy graphics on the sides of their trucks or trailers. Something as easy as remembering the company website, printed on the truck may be all you need to hook up to phone numbers, street addresses, and maybe even a job application. You see these trucks at sporting events, fairs, conventions, trade shows, and just about anywhere there are people. These fancy rigs are fancy for one reason only. They want people to see them.

Keep in mind; these companies are often looking for drivers that can relate well to their sometimes executive and even celebrity clientele. Certain drivers are not in this category and might not present themselves as a good fit for the company. You often see such folks wandering around the video game room at the truck stop or just milling about the rest rooms, not really doing anything of consequence. Touring companies are not looking for an unkempt, foul smelling scrounge. Bet on it.

The well groomed (as in the clean shaven, showered, and with a reasonably recent haircut look, and with clean neat clothing) are not going to be frowned upon as offensive. Perhaps you are only a tour truck driver. You still need to be viewed as a professional and the image you impart as a representative for your company is essential. You are probably NOT going to be dealing with your average warehouse cretins or dock workers, thus you don't need or want to be perceived in a similar vein. Keep this in mind. It is relevant to your success in touring. Truck drivers generally do not fare well on the social scale. It is up to you to change that perception.

It is most assured that you do not need to look like a model, but I guarantee you, that personal appearance does matter. Sell yourself as being what they are looking for and you too could be kickin' back and groovin' on the 43rd floor of the Westin Hotel in downtown Seattle, sleepin' in the "Heavenly Bed" instead of the back of your rig, and dining on sushi or steak at the local bistro. "Hell yes!" It is out there and available to those that put out the effort. Don't miss out on the incredible opportunity for the best driving jobs of all.

This little volume of stories of exciting travel to fun places, life altering experiences, and riveting adventures on the road of life is for one thing. It is to "get your mind right" (Right out of "Cool Hand Luke"). By reading this you should be able to see your way clear to checking out the world of a "professional tourist." Can you do this or not? The answer is most likely "YES," but only if you are willing to make the effort. As that great philosopher, vocalist, entertainer, and radio announcer extraordinaire David Lee Roth said, "Jump! Go ahead and jump." Do it now and if it doesn't work out for you, well you can blame me later for all of it. "Thanks a lot."

See ya in the wind. Out.

Breinigsville, PA USA
18 November 2009
227771BV00003B/19/A